MICROCOSM · PUBLISHING

MICROCOSM PUBLISHING is Portland's most diversified publishing house and distributor with a focus on the colorful, authentic, and empowering. Our books and zines have put your power in your hands since 1996, equipping readers to make positive changes in their lives and in the world around them. Microcosm emphasizes skill-building, showing hidden histories, and fostering creativity through challenging conventional publishing wisdom with books and bookettes about DIY skills, food, bicycling, gender, self-care, and social justice. What was once a distro and record label started by Joe Biel in a drafty bedroom was determined to be *Publisher's Weekly's* fastest growing publisher of 2022 and has become among the oldest independent publishing houses in Portland, OR and Cleveland, OH. We are a politically moderate, centrist publisher in a world that has inched to the right for the past 80 years.

Global labor conditions are bad, and our roots in industrial Cleveland in the 70s and 80s made us appreciate the need to treat workers right. Therefore, our books are MADE IN THE USA.

CONTENTS

PUNK WOMEN

DAVID A. ENSMINGER

40 YEARS OF MUSICIANS WHO BUILT PUNK ROCK

MICROCOSM PUBLISHING
Portland, OR ⚲ Cleveland, OH

PUNK WOMEN
40 YEARS OF MUSICIANS WHO BUILT PUNK ROCK

© 2021 David A. Ensminger
© This edition Microcosm Publishing 2021
First edition - 3,000 copies - May 11, 2021
Second Printing, February 2023
ISBN 978-1-62106-551-7
This is Microcosm #588
Design and Cover by Sonny Kay and Joe Biel
Edited by Sarah Koch
Cover photos of Bikini Kill in Minot, North Dakota by Brent Braniff
Pages 17-23, 178-182 originally appeared in *Razorcake*
Pages 156-158, 164-173 previously published versions appeared in *Popmatters*
Pages 173-177 previously appeared in *Houston Press*

To join the ranks of high-class stores that feature Microcosm titles, talk to your local rep: In the U.S. **COMO** (Atlantic), **ABRAHAM** (Midwest), **BOB BARNETT** (Texas, Oklahoma, Louisiana), **IMPRINT** (Pacific), **TURNAROUND** (Europe), **UTP/MANDA** (Canada), **NEW SOUTH** (Australia/New Zealand), **GPS** in Asia, Africa, India, South America, and other countries, or **FAIRE** in the gift trade.

For a catalog, write or visit:
Microcosm Publishing
2752 N Williams tAve.
Portland, OR 97227
https://microcosm.pub/PunkWomen

Did you know that you can buy our books directly from us at sliding scale rates? Support a small, independent publisher and pay less than Amazon's price at **www.Microcosm.Pub**

Library of Congress Cataloging-in-Publication Data

Names: Ensminger, David A., author.
Title: Punk women : 40 years of musicians who built punk rock / David Ensminger.
Description: Portland : Microcosm Publishing, 2021. | Summary: "In this exhaustive anthology, David Ensminger delves underground to explore the oft overlooked community of badass women who shaped the punk scene. There is a common thread of women being excluded and gatekept from the hardcore music scene but this anthology challenges that notion and shows that women have still been able to overcome, kick ass, and shred alongside the best of them. Biographies, interviews, band anecdotes, and never-before-published photos showcase the talent and artistry of bands like Bikini Kill, The Glittersluts, Bratmobile, Spitboy, the Germs, The Slits, and dozens more. Through its intimate aesthetic analysis and raw zine-like presentation, this is an essential resource for anyone looking to discover, rediscover, and cherish punk history"-- Provided by publisher.
Identifiers: LCCN 2020054533 | ISBN 9781621065517 (paperback)
Subjects: LCSH: Women punk rock musicians. | Punk rock musicians. | Punk culture. | Riot grrrl movement. | Punk rock music--History and criticism.
Classification: LCC ML82 .E58 2021 | DDC 781.66092/52--dc23
LC record available at https://lccn.loc.gov/2020054533

A FOREWORD FROM KATY OTTO

I t matters so much to see yourself represented.

I grew up in the DC metropolitan area. I fell in love with music at an early age and this love grew to a fever pitch in high school. When I felt alienated, or depressed, or loney, I would lock myself in my room with Tori Amos, Nirvana, or Hole blasting. I would make audio cassettes of my favorite radio programs, and would record MTV's *120 Minutes* on VHS tapes to rewind and playback again and again.

At sixteen, my friends and I began putting on our own shows with local bands in VFW halls and church basements. I went to my first Fugazi show, and my world opened up. I had begun playing drums after going to Lollapalooza 1995 and seeing the inimitable Patty Schemel from Hole. Watching her play drums was the single most beautiful thing I had ever seen in my life. I wanted to access that strength and power, and it was seeing another woman do so that made me feel inspired and encouraged.

It turns out I was very lucky to live in the DC metropolitan area as a teenager. Our music scene was extraordinary, the stuff of legends—and it was populated heavily by some of the most impressive, prolific, and accessible women imaginable. Punk in DC was fueled by women. They were front and center—writing zines, playing in bands, putting out records, curating shows.

I formed my first band Bald Rapunzel with another teenage girl, Bonnie Schlegel. We'd play together in that band for five years, touring the country, releasing records, and eventually founding our own record label with our other friend Sara Klemm in 2000. Bonnie named it Exotic Fever Records to connote that which is infectious and rare. Bonnie came up with the idea to start a label—she believed strongly in a number of bands and wanted to do all she could to help them get a fair shot at gaining an audience. She enlisted my help, and we looped Sara Klemm in too. However, we didn't exactly know how to run a record label—and that is where the amazing women of DC punk would come in.

Kim Coletta, interviewed in this book, was our mentor. She answered our phone calls, spent tremendous time with us, and walked us through various processes with a generosity of spirit which was unmatched—all while her own band Jawbox was signing to a major label and touring, and while she was running her own label DeSoto. In Kim, we saw someone to aspire to. We knew that women and girls controlling the means of production for punk and DIY culture mattered. She helped us to feel confident and like we belonged. We also had great resources created by Kristin Thomson and Jenny Toomey, two women in our community who ran the label Simple Machines and put out a zine that served as a guide to how to put out your own seven inch. We were encouraged in our own band by Kathy Cashel and Jen Semo, two brilliant musicians from our favorite band Norman Mayer Group who came out to our shows to cheer us on. Everywhere we looked, women in our community were making things happen, and were helping the younger women coming after them.

Early on, *Seventeen* Magazine contacted Dischord Records, where Kim also worked, and asked if they knew of any young women running record labels. They mentioned us, and we were featured in the magazine. This helped us to grow our project. In 2020, Exotic Fever Records celebrated twenty years with a virtual festival streamed worldwide. We've released over 65 items to date, including five benefit compilations raising funds for the DC Books to Prisons, Vietnam Veterans of America Benefits Program, Compassion Over Killing, the District Alliance for Safe Housing, and Helping Individual Prostitutes Survive. Over time, young women and girls began asking us questions—and we tried to pay it forward by helping them as much as we could.

I am thrilled at the release of this book, which tells the story of many women from the punk and DIY community. I remember the thrill I felt as a young woman seeing The Muffs, and how heartbroken I was to hear of the passing of their legendary frontwoman Kim Shattuck in 2019. We hear from her here. I was awestruck years ago to play a show with Mecca Normal with my own band Trophy Wife, and as I near my 43rd birthday I am grateful to hear from Jean Smith about the ways in which older women are received in the subculture—and why it's critically important that we remain there as creative agents.

In Philadelphia, where I have made my home for the past ten years, I have been deeply fortunate to experience extraordinary contributions to punk by badass women/queer/gender noncomforing people of color. I have also seen punk forms of expression across a range of genres—afrofuturist sci-fi, dance, visual art, soundscapes, and more. I hope we all continue to support art that stretches and expands across these kinds of borders and boundaries. I hope this book helps people to understand how vital women's voices are to a musical ecosystem. Finally, I look forward to being astounded and transported by the women and girls yet to come. The future is yours and our ears are wide open.

This book is an invaluable way to help keep the home fires burning for a form of expression which helped me form my identity.

AN INTRODUCTION FROM THE AUTHOR

For four decades, women have often been ignored or marginalized in the history of punk despite being an intrinsic and vital part of the movement since the very first whispers of "year zero." A few years ago, I published this book in two slim volumes as a do-it-yourself effort in order to shed light on their essential involvement and honor their musical legacies while exploring the veins of pop culture as well. Following the original publication, I hoped that someone else would take up the cause and create a more comprehensive collection. In the absence of other attempts, Microcosm Publishing has afforded me the opportunity to expand and clarify the content, which is not meant to supply copious biographical matter. Instead, I am keen to explore these women's enduring music, sensibilities, and artistry.

Since the 1980s, I have typed up, torn up, and copied and pasted fanzines, contributed to underground press galore (*Trust*, *Artcore*, *Maximum Rocknroll*, *Razorcake*, and many more), built and maintained websites and blogs, plus penned academic books and Internet columns and articles (*Houston Press*, *Popmatters*). In addition, I have shot thousands of photographs and Xeroxed homemade gig flyers, sketched fiery poems, and played alongside a retinue of bold and blazoning women hell-bent on squashing rulebooks. With the help of my decades-long research and firsthand accounts by those I have contacted, I hope to reveal segments of punk's murky past. By capturing a wide scope of performers from classic three-chord punk and grunge/garage/gunk to Riot Grrrl, post-hardcore, and emo, in this short compendium I have tried to use a varied, democratic, and inclusive perspective ranging from discussing totally obscure bands to limelighters. As such, it also explores issues at stake: social and gender politics, rampant violence, reproductive rights, modern feminism, genre categories, sexual norms, war and technology, the record industry and tour networks, DIY causes, humanitarian values, media narratives, street level power struggles, and much more.

I freely admit that this book is incomplete. I do not spend space on Hole, Runaways, L7, Pandoras, Go-Go's, etc. So, it is imperfect and subjective, for it is a product of me, essentially. In some cases, it offers a conversation with the women themselves, sometimes within recent months, sometimes from deep in my archives. I structured it more or less like a fanzine: I want the text to bombard readers, so they wrestle with language, logic, and description.

I did not attempt a tightly segmented, linear, comparttmentalized sense of organization. Instead, I mix and match eras, genres and styles, generations and subcultures, politics and people, as well as regions and places: hopefully, through such random association, new linkages, bridges, and relationships can arise. Think of the text as a sort of cut-up method in sections, or a stream-of-consciousness, or an estrangement effect on-the-go in an effort to prove history is messy and multi-layered.

In the end, I simply sought to excavate the wild ones—the ones with sharpened brazenness, and to shatter the quietude of writing. This is a jolting, feverish journey, I hope.

—David Ensminger, April 2017/ February 2021.

Neighborhood Brats, 2019, by David Ensminger

THE MUFFS

If some punk felt like endless nocturnal emissions of ennui uttered from the white, male suburban wasteland, the Muffs were the full-blare scream from the heart of the city. As arbiters of growling rock'n'punk under the tutelage of singer and guitarist Kim Shattuck, who passed in Oct. 2019, they offer a terrific meld of thrusting Northwest musical character (on tunes like the sludge pop of "Lucky Guy") à la bands like Monomen and Nirvana, and sometimes snide and bratty bubblegum vibes akin to the Queers ("Oh Nina" and "Agony"). They embodied ragged girl rock glory, from the Runaways to the Pandoras (of which Shattuck was a member), traits ignited on tunes like the molten, drum-splattered "No Action." For lighter doses, try "Take a Take a Me."

Since the demise of *Flipside*, they have remained a band central to the zine's arms-wide-open retinue. They symbolize a Los Angeles-style rock'n'roll that is irreverent, beset by humor, and a welcomed antidote to the serial severity of punk's choleric crowds. In doing so, they have more in tune with early British punkers like the Damned, the Lurkers, and the Boys than the often grim-faced moral authorities of hardcore.

Like the Fastbacks from Seattle, the Muffs was a band existing in long-lived operation mode for decades; through the ups and down, pinwheel curves and industry flare-ups, including the guitar-driven indie rock 1990s and technological meltdowns, when CDs became a metallic garbage heap. They were survivors, true

Photo Credit: Alison Dyer

spirits, unabashed loyalists, and the beachside vibes of "Forget the Day" feel like wistful postcards from another era, just as "Brand New Chevy" pictures a hot rod heaven for greasy girls.

They do not exude the melodrama of Hole or the eureka art visions of Yeah Yeah Yeahs. In contrast, they offer workaday world songs rooted in jukebox punk for smart, angry, pop culture saturated teens, but the tunes also sit in the heart of plenty of wayward adults. So, when the Muffs unleashed their version of "Kids in America," perhaps their 'blockbuster,' despite its mainstream sheen (don't forget, Kim Wilde harnessed James Stevenson of Gen X for the original's appealing guitar), they turned it into a horse-rasp of potent dismay-meets-aggro. As such, it constitutes a warning: the kids *are not* alright.

Kim Shattuck

I don't know if my being a woman is why I wasn't taken seriously by Reprise when I announced I wanted to produce our third record *Happy Birthday to Me* in 1997 or if it's because I had very little to no experience as a producer. Either way, I am very stubborn, strong-willed, and was getting extremely tired of fighting with producers to get the sound I wanted for our band. They agreed to let me do it, but they insisted it would be credited as "Produced by The Muffs."

Still, I jumped at that because I knew Ronnie and Roy wouldn't do anything, so it would be me as producer. And since I didn't have any real experience, I took that chance to learn and do it myself. We ended up using the amazing engineers Steve Holroyd (who first worked at Marquee Studios overseas—with Elton John, etc.—then at Ocean Way Recording in L.A.) and Sally Browder (the Joykiller, New Model Army, the Red Aunts), and the first thing I learned was: you are only as good as your engineer. That's a fact.

I don't know why I once said I preferred the Pistols to the Clash. I like a few Clash songs, and I like a few Sex Pistols songs. It made me sad that stupid Sid Vicious got all the attention. He was so terrible. Blondie, though, is amazing. Much better than the Clash and the Pistols. Really, my motto has always been "It's all about the melody."

We were asked to do one of three songs for the movie *Clueless*. We picked the most melodic song out of the three.

The Beat (with Paul Collins) song that we covered, "Rock N Roll Girl," was for a compilation, maybe for Planned Parenthood. I thought it would be funny to sing the words differently in that song. Since the lyrics were, "I wanna be with a rock

The Muffs

LUNACHICKS

WATERDOG

SUNDAY SEPTEMBER 10TH

DV8

a private club for members

doors 7:00 $8

and roll girl," which I totally thought were stupid lyrics, I decided to sing it as, "I want to beat up a rock and roll girl." Well, that didn't sit so well with the organization who was putting out the record, since they basically help battered women, so they asked me to re-sing the choruses. The nerve!

There's room for all kinds of different styles. I'm not petty about that kind of shit. I've always felt that we were our own thing and not really a part of any one scene.

I love the Dickies and the Groovie Ghoulies, but I also love other genres too. I think we are closer in spirit to some of those mid-1960s British Invasion bands, except we have extremely loud guitars. In the case of the Red Hot Chili Peppers, I just hated their style. I had nothing against them personally. Flea is super-nice and a great bassist. I have nothing against them now, either. But at the time we were forming, they were super-popular, and their music was everywhere. Naturally, they became, for me, something to aspire against.

Some of our more eye-popping posters, especially the Bogart's one, were done by Coop (Nirvana, Boss Hog, Nashville Pussy). He is the best in my opinion. His fetish stuff never offended me. I always got a kick out of it.

Heck, if you wanna be fair, then do a poster of a guy wearing heels standing around with a whip in his hand. You can show off his crotch bulge. That would be a good switcheroo. Fair is fair.

MECCA NORMAL

Jean Smith is half of the powerful, prolific, and poetry-infused duo Mecca Normal, whose uncanny, bare-boned punk helped paved the way for Riot Grrrl's forceful attack on gender norms and its embodiment of DIY punk production. Her one-of-a-kind vocal delivery, postmodern storytelling, and incisive intimacy make her a true maverick.

Stretching over thirteen albums alongside musical partner David Lester, who channels power chords and jazz riffs with ease and gusto, the two have plowed through the decades since the mid-1980s, leaving behind a slew of work that blurs the boundaries between genres. Meanwhile, her ongoing painting and novels have earned her much praise and a cult following as well.

Jean Smith

After we opened three big shows on the west coast for The Julie Ruin in October, 2016, I was ready to do more shows with cheering audiences of feminists who yelled out things like "you're the best!" between our songs which inadvertently represented each of the four decades that Mecca Normal has been writing, performing and recording feminist and anti-authoritarian lyrics.

Mecca Normal (Jean Smith & David Lester), Yo Yo a Gogo Festival in Olympia, Washington, 1994. Photo by Jeff Smith

It was incredible to listen to Kathleen Hanna on stage during their set telling the audience how important Mecca Normal had been to her and her friends—the women who went on to form Bikini Kill and Riot Grrrl. She also told them I was a great painter and that they should follow me on social media! I actually wondered if I was dreaming as I listened to her say my singing and lyrics were better than ever. Keyboard player Kenny Mellman said Mecca Normal was his favorite band! I mean, maybe he meant when he was a young gay guy in San Francisco in the 80s and 90s. It was a real thrill to hear our work being put into this context considering most of our shows since 2000 have been extremely small with minuscule record sales, but fame and fortune have never been big motivators.

After the Vancouver show, The Julie Ruin wanted us to play the remainder of their west coast tour, but we found out at the Portland show that the booking agent couldn't make it happen. I have to admit it was weird to be locking up my apartment in Vancouver not knowing if I was going for the weekend or three weeks. There wouldn't be too many 57-year-old women in that position and it felt good to have maintained a life where that was even possible. Single and self-employed.

After the excitement of the shows, I got back into painting the $100 portraits that I sell on Facebook. Every month in 2016, I've sold enough paintings to pay my rent. In 2017, I'll divide my time between painting and writing a YA novel. I write literary fiction, but my agent specializes in YA, so I came up with a story about teens starting a punk band. I'll be portraying underground and all-ages scenes as the inspiring communities of creative collaborators that I know them to be, steering clear of random conflict and animosity between characters—especially female characters—that tend to drive mainstream plots.

David: Many people draw direct links between Mecca Normal and Riot Grrrl—although I might draw a stronger line between the band (who I always thought borrowed inspiration from Young Marble Giants and Lydia Lunch) and the work of PJ Harvey—albums like *Flood Plain* and her *4-Track Demos*, made the same year, seem like partners in creative crimes. Yet that is the meanderings of critics. If you feel part of a lineage, what is it?

Jean: I don't feel any particular shared lineage or affinity with PJ Harvey. It could be timing. We were fully immersed in writing, recording and touring. Mecca Normal is a conversation between a man and a woman who aren't romantically connected. Her music serves a very different function for her singing. Her uitar typically comes down to accommodate the singing. The whole is a singular demonstration of intensity produced by a solo operator. Listening to "Man-Size" as I write this. For all the rough edges, her orchestration is pretty slick. Nope, I just don't see the connection. She's a good guitar player, so that's good! She sounds like Patti Smith if Patti Smith could play the guitar, but then again, I'm not a big Patti Smith fan either.

David: I intended to mean, what legacy do you *actually feel part of*, if not her, or Patti Smith? Do you feel, as writers suggest, part of the Riot Grrrl movement? Or something else entirely, or none at all?

Jean: I feel directly inspired by the women in and around the London punk scene in the late 1970s. Raincoats, Au Pairs, Slits, CRASS, Poison Girls, X-Ray Spex, Hazel O'Connor. David lived—and squatted—in London during that time. He had a girlfriend who was in a punk band, and he managed to see a few of these bands—and Gang of Four—so he pointed me in this direction. He bought me a lot of these records in the early 1980s and we started Mecca Normal in 1984. I had a portable cassette deck and I went down to the industrial part of the waterfront in Vancouver in my 1970-something Toyota Corolla and sang along to "Warrior in Woolworths" (X-Ray Spex) and Lola (Raincoats) playing on a tape in the car stereo and recorded myself on the portable tape deck. I still have that tape!

We were well underway when Riot Grrrl started. I'd been married and divorced, basically. I wasn't a "girl" at all and I'd done my fair share of educating people about the "political incorrectness" of calling women girls, so I was hardly going to join anything with "girl" in it. Plus, I don't join anything anyway.

Mecca Normal is an acknowledged inspiration to the co-founders of Riot Grrrl. Kathleen Hanna has said there wouldn't be a Bikini Kill if there wasn't a Mecca Normal. When Fader.com asked who had influenced her in the early days, Kathleen said, "Lyrically, Jean Smith from Mecca Normal. She was really poetic and had feminist ideas at the core of a lot of her songs and she wasn't ashamed of it. She wrote a song about street harassment and the male gaze, and she played at a feminist art gallery that my friend and I started. And when I saw her, I was just like, that's it. I'm done."[1]

I mean, it's a bit weird to, all these years later, still be describing myself as an inspiration to founders of Riot Grrrl and a much better known musician, but I set myself up for that. That's what we wanted to do from the very beginning! That was our specific purpose—to inspire young women to form bands with their friends, to write, and to sing lyrics about their experience.

David: In a *Wondering Sound* interview, you told Tobi Vail, "We're minuscule on the radar of mainstream people," but in essence, has this allowed a certain kind of anonymity and freedom to pursue music without a sense of having to please . . . ?

Jean: Well, Mecca Normal was never saddled with the need to please, that's for sure! It was an urge to agitate. And to educate on everything from sexism and violence against women to poverty, housing rights and the woes of capitalism. I come from a creative background. Both parents are painters. Abstract expressionists. No need to please involved there! I grew up listening to their jazz, which included Bill Evans, Oscar Peterson, Keith Jarrett, etc.—a fair few pianists, not so many vocalists. Jazz never struck me as a need to please situation either. It felt highly impulsive and hinged to the emotional landscape of the individual.

Concurrently, I was exposed to the formulation of the advertising industry because my father was an ad agency art director (circa *Mad Men*) who went from Vancouver

Mecca Normal (Jean Smith & David Lester) by Judith Baumann

to N.Y.C. to work with top photographers from *Vogue*, etc., and top models. So, I was behind the scenes in the very need-to-please world of illusion that is advertising. Where the final product—the ad—is a highly-contrived manipulation with a specific purpose—to sell shit to people. From a very early age, I watched how models were used. How light and language were used. How psychological weaknesses were exploited—because these things were talked about and demonstrated. I've always been conscious that mystery is very appealing to the consumer. Take your Jandeks or your Salingers, for instance. I've always gone out of my way to say way more than necessary and to give the impression of being both angry and completely transparent—all of which is distasteful, especially in a woman. Generating this stance has protected us from excessive interest and allowed us to move freely in both physical and creative realms. No one is depending on us to make a living, like a road crew or a label.

There's this cool little space you can carve out for yourself if you're not hell-bent on being popular or making a bunch of money. It has more to do with functioning within a community of like-minded people than it does fortune and fame. It has more to do with the reason for making art, a reason other than fame. Although, having said all that, I would still like things to be easier for Dave and I financially, but I feel there's a big shove from younger generations that older people should just go away because they had their turn and now they're just taking up space and what could they possibly have to say that would be interesting? It's weird, because older people don't want to draw attention to their age. We're all supposed to be trying our damnedest to cover up any signs of aging. From grey hair to wrinkles—to be old is very, very, VERY BAD! To be an older person is a cultural taboo. You are a drag. Your body is disgusting. For young people, it's all out in the open. You hear them mocking older people, talking about how irritating they are. It's a prejudice that's not being acknowledged or challenged along with racism, gender issues, and feminism. I think it's too scary for most older people. I think they're happy to be invisible to avoid being abused and exploited by younger people. Humans have a nasty tendency to pick on the vulnerable.

I saw a thread on my Facebook feed written by a young woman who does sex work. She asked her friends if they would have sex with a disgusting old man for $5,000. Most were grossed out, but said they would. Some said no way. I wanted to ask how old she was talking about, but to them, in their early 20s, I guess that could be a guy in his 40s, 50s, 60s or who knows? Just the idea that prostitutes are loath to take $5,000 to have sex with a disgusting "old man" is interesting. Although, I totally recall when I was in my early 40s, the idea of having sex with a 50-year-old man was disgusting, but then, when it happened (some years later), it wasn't too bad! Aging is weird.

David: I almost want to title this interview "Aging is weird." It's so true, for me as well.

Jean: As a musician—or someone culturally significant in a previous era—when you get into your 50s, especially as a woman, people start acting like your time was some other time, except that you're still standing there with a bunch of ideas and the need to make work and money, but suddenly it's like you're a museum piece. There's this strange assumption that you have always been old and therefore you know how to be old, that you must know how to get what you need, that you have it all together, because that was the gist of it all, right? You get your education or training, make your way upwards through a profession, build equity, have the family and then you're somehow set. None of this is true if you deviate from the start and go in another direction—like starting a band based in confronting social injustices. I own nothing. No car, no house. Nothing valuable. I don't have a partner or kids. I don't stand to inherit any particularly large amount. I'll be selling my parents' 1970-something single-wide trailer after they die and splitting the proceeds with my brother.

Right now, I'm making ends meet painting $100 portraits. I would say this is one of the happiest times

Mecca Normal (Jean Smith & David Lester)
Vera in Groningen, Holland, 1995. Photo by Snorkel

in my life. To be making and selling art—enough to live on! It's incredible! I started painting self-portraits when I was 13 and have continued over the years. I've tried to paint at least one a year, every year since, but I had no idea there was a market for faces. Anonymous faces which are more about the actual paint—the composition, style, color—and human emotions, I suppose, than any sort of urge to depict a specific face. I've sold paintings to instructors from the Yale School of Art and the Art Institute of Chicago, painters whose work has been exhibited in the Museum of Modern Art and the Whitney Biennial, and by art critics for *Artforum* and the *Winnipeg Free Press*. Johanna Fateman (formerly of Le Tigre) has been really enthusiastic and helpful in pointing artists she knows in my direction. Julie Dioron and Rose Melberg have bought them as part of the 60 plus sales directly from my Facebook page. I think people want to buy directly from the artist. Skip the art dealers and galleries, etc.

David: For half a decade, you worked at Curves, and more recently within the food industry, working via a facade or persona (as many of us do) so you can make the art you want, on the terms you desire. But in what ways does the emphasis on bodily health, attention to nutrition, and fulfilling art intersect in unsuspecting ways in your life?

Jean: I started weightlifting in 1979, so I recently celebrated 35 years working out in community gyms in Vancouver. It's the type of workout that suits me. Aggressive, solo, ego-based, and fast. I was 19 when I started, and I don't recall any other women at the facility I went to. Prior to that, I'd been a ski instructor. My mother was very

Jean Smith and David Lester by Pat Blashill, 1990.

health-conscious, and she shared a lot of information about nutrition with me as a kid. To this day, I eat what I need to eat, loosely based on the original food guide.

The Curves job was great because it was very physical, and it involved teaching and training both staff and clients, and it was very social. I could talk about the novels I was writing and, at that time, song lyrics were directly out of those novels. Working at the gourmet food store was kind of depressing. Most of my co-workers were all wrapped up in what was delicious and not what was healthy. So, I tried to keep quiet about my beliefs. If I told someone I had kale for dinner after the gym, they'd look at me like I was less than something on the bottom of their shoe. The enemy.

As far as how being creative and maintaining a healthy lifestyle intersect in unsuspecting ways, I'd have to ask, unsuspecting to whom? I've been using physical activity and nutrition to maintain mental and physical health so long that nothing about the benefits are unexpected.

When I turned 40, I quit drinking. At that point I had to sort of reframe daily life with more emphasis on nutrition and getting to the gym. It was helpful to work at a gym for some of those years!

David: You opened for Fugazi, and have recognized the limited audience you might speak to, as if "preaching to the choir," but yet Ian MacKaye himself told me, "It's not preaching to the converted that's important, it's what the converted do. I have no problem with preaching to the converted, because then the converted can go out and kick some ass." Would you agree?

Jean: Opening for Fugazi was definitely not preaching to the choir for us! I don't think I've ever talked about kicking ass. I started Mecca Normal specifically to change the world. To encourage young women to get together with their friends and start bands in which they wrote and performed lyrics about their experiences as women in music and society. This happened. It was called Riot Grrrl. If that's preaching to the converted so the converted can go out and kick some ass, then yes.

David: Vic Bondi of Articles of Faith says he expects backlash against women if Hillary Clinton becomes President, just as racism and intolerance recently peaked under Obama's two terms. Your bandmate David told Tobi, "in terms of misogyny and the state of sexism in the world . . . it's frightening that very little has changed." Might her presence as President, even disregarding her politics, reveal an ugly side of North American life?

Jean: Backlash against women? Women are in the position of perpetual backlash every fucking day of their lives in every part of the world. Are the existing conditions of sexism going to be exposed and attended to during a Clinton administration? Ideally. Is that going to make some men angry? Yes. When the systemic oppression of women is addressed, it seems likely that some men will mock and attack women more openly, but it won't be like we didn't know that this is already a pervasive, underlying mindset. When men are frightened or hurt they tend to get angry and violent. Looking for connections between any sort of peak in racism during the Obama administration is complex. The criminalization of black life has a much longer arc.

David: By the 1990s, you jumped deeply into writing and began focusing on tightened language that could, as you told Tobi, "transcend and almost become invisible." In

Mecca Normal/*Jarred Up*: songs from compilations and singles
(K Records, 1993). Album cover design by Jean Smith.

turn, did that affect your songwriting style as well—a newfound attention to both detail and condensed narratives? For me, I felt that might be apparent on songs like "1922" and the vivid, vulnerable song/vignette "Attraction is Ephemeral," which made my mind recall Earnest Hemingway or Raymond Carver.

Jean: Thanks for mentioning Raymond Carver! He's one of my favourite writers. "1922" is from 2006's "The Observer" which is basically an album about my online dating adventures. As for how it and "Attraction is Ephemeral" (from the same album) were written, they feel very similar in their story-telling nature. "1922" is more abstract even though it involves a world-building aspect. Actually, I guess both songs place the characters in physical situations. Both songs express a sense of injustice at the way women are treated by men.

In "Attraction," it's within a male/female relationship dynamic, when one person (the man) is of a professional class and the other (the woman) is of an artist class. In "1922" we go back to when women had no clout as artists. To a time when it was all about how the male artist dominated the women in his life. The two songs are bookends, in a way, describing nuances of the overarching condition that feminism addresses.

I wrote "1922" while David played guitar. With "Attraction" I had the lyrics typed out before we began playing. I always record what we do so we can go from what happened in the first take, which is often very close to how we want it. I have tapes (and now files) of almost every one of our rehearsals. I need a variety of ways to write good songs. I'd hate it if it was formulaic. I will say that some of our best songs are written on the first time, through—which is why I wish we had a better way to record. I'd love to have a great studio setup.

David: I know David's book about Emma Goldman is partly about documenting the life of a radical who ended up in Toronto, but also spent fifty years struggling for basic human rights. As someone who has also spent decades defining, and re-defining, your music, feminism, and sense of anarchism, does her life or work mean much to you as well?

Jean: David and I are very different people. I'm more into either documenting my own experiences or inventing characters to use in the process of clarifying thoughts about personalities in relation to society and other personalities. The portrait paintings I'm doing now are an extension of the way I build and use characters in novels and songs. I get to know them by constructing them and defining them through linguistic, musical and visual intensities.

David, I believe, is more interested in re-framing and expressing aspects of existing history.

I wrote and directed a stage adaption for David's last graphic novel. *The Listener* is about a political artist who went to Europe to regroup after an unsettling incident. She met an elderly couple who told her a little-known story about how Hitler came to power. It was great to go into classrooms and libraries and run through our live performance in character and then, at the end, we sort of fall out of character and become Mecca Normal.

Emma Goldman's life and work don't mean anything to me. I'm not planning on playing the role of a dumpy, unattractive woman wearing 19-whatever garb. So, I'm not sure what's up with that. We haven't really talked about creating a stage adaptation for this book. It seems unlikely.

David: You've worked with a spate of labels, including K, Matador, and Kill Rock Stars. Do you see a place for such labels in the future, or were they, in some ways, a means to an end? Albeit, in rare cases, like Kill Rock Stars, they also fostered a sense of community. Now that a band can Periscope their live gigs in real-time and record an entire album on GarageBand and disseminate it on Bandcamp (where Dischord just dumped their whole catalog), are labels passé?

Jean: I'd say the communities around K Records were solid around the time we were on the label, as were what we knew of the Matador community. Maybe less with them— being on the West Coast made it different for us—but I think there was some sense of community there. The type of discussion that swirls around labels would be missed. Albeit, conversation in recent years seems to be about differences and difficulties.

Bands have been able to record and manufacture albums on their own—as we did— it's really about the means of dissemination and promotion. That's what you need a label for. You need a way to get it out there—which, if that's Bandcamp, then you need a way to get it to stand out, and that's usually what the label can generate with the media. It always looks better to have someone else saying how great your band is, even when it's your label. They are your label because they love what you do, so losing that element is a hindrance on many levels.

We tend to be fairly D.I.Y. on the publicity side of things—sending out press releases and setting up interviews—getting content out there to promote our music and other projects. We can't afford to tour extensively because not enough people come out to our shows. Everything changed for almost everyone around 2000, with Napster and file sharing, and fewer people going out to shows in general. We were significant at a certain point within a few different communities, but we didn't want to stop after that point. We didn't come to a natural end point and move on to other professions. I didn't have a back-up plan, and any success Mecca Normal had was a total surprise. Getting a four out of five star review—and named a "Band to Watch" along with Radiohead and Liz Phair—in *Rolling Stone*? Didn't see it coming.

David: Your life is a panorama of output—a painting carer, a writing career, then, of course, the band's continuum . . . but literally, how do you stay afloat in the 21st century, when making art in a digital world, as just mentioned, can be difficult at best?

Jean: I spend a lot of time online—on social media, writing novels, updating various pages, and now, selling paintings. I create and maintain websites [on] WordPress for various projects. I've made hundreds of videos and posted them on YouTube and Vimeo. But, until now—with the paintings—nothing has really worked, in terms of attracting enough people to make a living. Not that money is at the root of what I do, but I am currently painting to avoid taking another part-time job in retail. The last job was in a Home Depot garden center and, as a part time employee, they had me scheduled seven days in a row for 5:00 a.m. shifts to haul water for about twice as many hours as I needed or wanted. I told them I wasn't available at that time of day, every day of the week. They ignored me. So I quit. The paintings were starting to take off, and I decided to keep painting. Jen (of the band Submission Hold) called the paintings "a perfect storm" when I started selling between 9 and 12 a month. It's the low price, the size—11 x 14"—and something about the faces that resonate with people—which I think has a lot to do with the time spent and the intensity of writing about characters in my novels. When you have to make that leap from imagination to words, you formulate something that will work for your readers.

Then, later, to start painting portraits—which is something I've done since I was 13—I tapped into capturing micro-expressions and nuances of emotion in the same way I might reveal them in a story. I paint from photographs I like, mostly women. Some of them are people you might know of, but I'm not all caught up in realistic representations of specific people. Famous people have better photos of themselves! Better lighting! If I'm painting a model in a traditional fashion photo, there is something about that revealed in my painting—where the make-up meets bare skin, an awareness that is not quite hidden. I have painted quite a few of a particular trans model and many others are intentionally ungendered. For me, it's about the act of painting more than the final evidence of that time spent painting. In any one painting, there might be many variations that occur before I finally stopped. With painting, it's knowing when to stop. My subject's character begins to form when I start painting. I edit constantly, changing intensity around the mouth and the eyes, altering the style—combining loose and realistic features, forcing the viewer's brain to fill in missing details—honing an impression of who they are becoming, who I'm making them.

David: The band has waned a bit here and there over the years, and you've both jumped to side projects, but how do you maintain that core productivity and freshness?

Jean: David and I have an excellent creative partnership. When interest in Mecca Normal fell off, we both had areas we wanted to put attention into. For him it's graphic novels and for me it was writing. As a woman, when I got into my 50s I started to feel invisible. In music especially, it's always about the new band. Young bands. Young women. When you're in your 50s, no one really cares what you're up to unless you've already made it somehow. Unless you're Melissa Etheridge or someone, it's pretty hopeless. I could be bitter, but we didn't set out to be part of any existing system or to succeed in any other way than in changing the world—which we did. I've never felt like my creativity had to manifest only through music.

Since there is no money coming my way from any sort of royalties or sales and no money from anything I write, I was a bit stuck in having to take part time jobs where I was lucky enough to be hired as an older person. I don't have an income otherwise. That's what's been so great about the paintings selling and why I'm hoping I can find a way to make it continue. If I can't, I have to work in a store—or I don't know, really. Jobs are tight here in Vancouver and it's a very expensive city, so it's an ongoing concern since I rent. I have to earn about $1,000 U.S.D. every month somehow. I have eight more years before I can collect the old age pension. So, if people aren't interested in my band, even though we still put out albums (the last one was produced by Kramer) and are into touring and my voice is probably better than ever, but we're excluded because I have been alive too long to be of interest.

I spent most of my time since 2000 writing novels and working part time. I was fortunate to have several businesses I worked at close, and so I was eligible for unemployment insurance. That was perfect. I got a lot of writing done. I have a literary agent working on selling one of them to a publisher and I've just started another one. And, in April, I quit my part time job to paint full time. I've sold over 60 paintings from my Facebook page in the past 6 months. It was originally just sort of a off-hand comment borne out of desperation. The part time job wasn't working out and I said I'd rather just paint 5 $100 paintings a day and sell them on Facebook. It turns out that there is a market for the portraits I've been doing. I wasn't planning on doing portraits for $100, because they should be significantly higher, but due to the crossed wires on what I said I was going to paint, people started snapping up the portraits as soon as I posted then, so I stuck with it and it continues to be a viable way to make a living. I like the direct from-the-artist model and making them a price that regular people can actually afford.

David: How much of the band was shaped by the particular politics and music of Vancouver, not just the legacy of Subhumans, DOA, Pointed Sticks, Modernettes, Dishrags, etc.?

Jean: Mecca Normal started because there were very few women in bands at the time Dave and I were going to shows in the early 80s (after the era you refer to). The politics that swirled around the scene definitely infused us with a specific awareness, but feminism was missing from the equation. It was weird because the Vancouver punk scene was sort of based on London, I'd say, and the London scene had a lot of women in it. Vancouver was pretty much a four-guys-on-stage, and when we started doing shows, people didn't like us, so we went on tour and found that people in other cities really liked us! We did two nights in an anarchist café in Montreal and got standing ovations—it was positively weird! San Francisco, Los Angeles, and New York City were great! If we'd fit into the scene in Vancouver, we might not have left and found what was out there beyond the city we both grew up in. When we got a lousy review in MRR, I realized we weren't going to be able to contribute to the hardcore scene. What we found was infinitely more interesting. It's all about tenacity and being flexible within parameters that may need to be adjusted over time.

We'd only played a handful of shows at the point when we went into a studio in 1985 to mix tapes we'd made on our Fostex four-track in a garage. After we released our first album (on our record label) someone "in the scene" said we shouldn't have released it because there were bands more deserving than us. I recall someone saying that we hadn't paid our dues. That phrase really stuck with me. From time to time, 30 years and 16 albums later, I still wonder if I've paid my dues.

Lisafer of 45 Grave, DI, Lisafer, Nina Hagen, and Screech of Death

Lisafer (Lisa Pifer) has been a punk devotee since the 1980s, though a grievous leg injury kept her from performing until the next decade. In the 1990s, she was an integral part of the rebirth of punk-as-mass-phenomenon in Los Angeles, where she became a member in the crunchy, hammering, punk-as-hell outfit Snap-Her, who appeared on the front cover of *Flipside* in Nov. 1995 and were signed to New Red Archives (run by Nicky Garratt of the UK Subs) but suffered a million line-up variations. Lisa provides the bass attack on their seminal single "We're Snap-Her . . . and You're Fucked," a tongue-in-cheek homage to the Meatmen. Their tunes are equally brutal, tasteless, rapacious, and cynical, from "I Hate Christmas" to "Fuck Earth Day," which applauds brown gaseous air, cut-down trees, gas guzzling cars, and aerosol fumes.

In essence, the band was a stye in the eye of political correctness—a lewd musical stew, an unsavory reaction to university clones. Yet they were a potent affront to stifling gender suppression as well, though more in line with Insaints and Plasmatics than

Riot Grrrl tirades. Pifer penned tunes that are shockingly humorous and dead-on, like "Penile Implant" ("taking steroids to get bigger why not get a penile implant!"), which crucifies machismo and links work-out culture to bodily dysfunction, and "Anal Retention," which abhors the lame, reactionary, uptight side of all people.

Pifer served as bass player in three internationally recognized seminal acts—45 Grave, DI, and Nina Hagen—as well as others, including her own venture Lisafer, featuring Rikk Agnew of the Adolescents. Among their triumphant take-aways is their rendition of "Police Car" by lauded street punk veterans Cockney Rejects (which they Americanize while adding doses of unkempt vitriol and pure energy) and their version of the titillating powder puff hit "Johnny Are You Queer?" first introduced by Josie Cotton in 1982. Other original tunes like "Positively Negative" are scorchers— rough, brash, and as hardcore as the Voids, while slower "Sex" reveals the dirty side of teenage "buttercups" being bamboozled into sex.

Upon moving to Texas a half-decade ago, she has remained committed to scorching, bratty, tongue-in-cheek, uber-Southern California style punk in Screech of Death, Austin legends The Next—a fixture since the 1970s—and the Guillotines. She approaches the world madly sincere, eyes wide open, sometimes straddling a shotgun, and remains feverishly committed to music. Underneath it all is a total kid at heart with a straight-forward attitude and tons of musical finesse at her fingertips.

Lisa Pifer

The first house I grew up in was in Chatsworth, CA, home of Spahn Movie Ranch (500 acre movie ranch off the Santa Susana Pass Road) and Charles Manson fame. Kitty-corner from us was James Lowe and his family, and my mom was a mentor to his wife, Pamela. He was the lead singer of the Electric Prunes, of "I Had Too Much To Dream (Last Night)" fame, so I got exposed to some amazing music right from the get-go.

In the late 1970s, a family moved in across the street and along with them came the Ramones. They were a wonderful Italian family, so loving: they fed me, took me in as their own, and exposed me to New York punk rock. Also, in junior high, I think I was about 13 or 14, Dave Grave of Voo-Doo Church (who featured Tina Winter on vocals) was the narc at my school. And every time I had an orthodontist appointment, he would ask me for my hall pass. I think everybody at my school was high on black beauties from Dave, which is hilarious, because his mom was the Spanish teacher. Those were different times.

Another factor for me getting intrigued by these different sounds, thoughts, and feelings was the fact that my friend's brother drummed for a band called Fatal Error in the early 1980s. And this so intrigued me because Fatal Error (who had one track on a Mystic Records compilation and were first named Symbolic Filth) is what used to come up on those old MS-DOS computers. Absolutely hilarious. Meanwhile, my other friend's brother was the first Mohican in our side of town, and I used to just sit and stare at him and think, *that is the most interesting specimen I have ever seen.*

Growing up in suburban Los Angeles was a trip. On Sunday nights, I listened to Rodney Bingenheimer KROQ—"Rodney on the ROQ." I think he was on late at night, but he exposed me to some really bad-ass shit that I'll never forget. It was thought-provoking, and I was always interested in the things outside the norm, being that I am outside the norm, in my brain.

Later on, when I moved to Hollywood, I used to play bass by myself in my apartment. Having grown up as a kid playing piano, I had what I call "forced piano lessons," but

I had no idea they would come in handy later on. I never wanted to play in a band, I wouldn't date guys that were in a band, because they cheat when they are on tour (hah hah!). My friends pretty much rolled me into band life like a gang. My first band was an all-girl unit called Snap-Her, and the fifth show I ever played in my life I became the bass player for Nina Hagen. She took out our little three-piece and added a second guitar player. We became Nina Hagen's back-up band. The rest, as they say, is her-story. And I have played with many great underground bands: I play drums,

David Ensminger

I play bass, and I play bass and sing reluctantly as the frontman of Screech of Death nowadays, plus sometimes moonlight with another beloved punk band in Austin called The Next.

I was also the only female player ever in DI, and I played drums for Alice Bag and Castration Squad for the 25th anniversary, and that line-up had Mary/Dinah Cancer of 45 Grave, Tiffany Kennedy, Tracy Lee, Alice, and myself. I did play bass in 45 Grave when Mary resurrected it in 2004 and toured with her in the states and Europe as well.

The Epoxies with Roxy Epoxy (Meredith DeLoca)

L ike an intergalactic punk squad, the Epoxies sprung from the grey pallor of Portland by training their ears on the past, the entire sweep of the Atari years, which they yanked forward in a manic panic spree that was well-fueled, purged of mawkishness, and born to run on electrodes and micro-processors. In doing so, they distilled bits of everyone: the 'future now' keyboard/synth insurrection of the Cars, Suicide, early Ultravox, and Devo; the dark otherworldy digital poetry of Gary Numan; and the frantic hurried beats, tongue-in-cheek humor, and indelible singalong blueprint of the Dickies. Sure, others like Servotron drilled away in this direction too, but they did not have Roxy Epoxy—the vamp of the binary void, a neo-synthetic Greta Garbo with a voice custom made from the remnants of well-worn Berlin, Motels, and Rezillos LPs. On some tunes, like the pulsing "My New World," the vibe is Yeah Yeah Yeahs (an art house romp that shakes with lyrical nods to a B-movie/sci-fi dimestore novel array), including a brave new world composed of "super-colliders ripping holes in space," "genetic disasters," "World War X," and the "walking dead"—all musically wrapped in laboratory-induced popping bass lines, exploding keyboards à la the Screamers, and a taut push-the-beat metronome drum urgency. In contrast, the moody "Here in the Dark" could have been a B-side of a Missing Persons single, for Epoxy's nocturnal croons are enough to make any jukebox turn to jelly.

Picked up by Fat Wreck Records, the kingdom of hummable, radio-friendly punk with panache and drive, they leapt to another level, especially on tunes like the uber-catchy *Synthesized*. In the video, the band may dress up as prefab, red-as-lipstick hot pants warriors that are exuberantly retro chic, but Epoxy's classic vocal delivery—

nervy, slightly robotic, deep with longing and tinged with machine era drama—is in perfect balance with the guitar's momentary nods to surf rock and pop-a-delic vibes hidden in the overall punk-ish assail. Similarly, *Everything Looks Beautiful on Video* is an uber-catchy ode to the dimming days of VHS, when material items (LPs, cassettes, transistor radios, VCRs, big screens) still held sway before the ether of the Internet took hold. Again, the synth solo creates bounce and sweet nostalgia, but Epoxy's plea, "electrify the airwaves / I'm on radio / you're so cruel to look away / somebody will love me here on video," steals the show.

Roxy began a regular DJ gig, fell in love with angular no wave, among other genres, and set up shop with the new band Roxy Epoxy and the Rebound, cutting the album Bandaids on Bullet Holes, which continued in the same vein as the Epoxies, especially on tight cuts like "1000," which is buffered by modulated bass'n'guitar lines, tactical and judicious synth, and Roxy's ever-present darkwave gravitas, while other tunes like *Spider and the Leach* are redolent with solemn post-punk hues—like a spectral fiction of a world gone mutant.

Roxy Epoxy / Meredith DeLoca

I discovered punk in the most amorphous ways. I knew it existed. I knew what it was. I was drawn to it, but I didn't have my friend's cool older brother or a random friend that could help me start to dig in.

In fact, I had "friends" who ridiculed me and called me a poser for my curiosity. They had started discovering punk about six months before me, so I spent time being ridiculed and trying to discover music on my own. This was around 1987, so I didn't have internet to help me out. At least I was somewhat thick-skinned to teasing by then, so it didn't matter much that I was being teased for something new.

I grew up in the Boston area, so my first big experiences with shows were the local hardcore scene. I've never been the girliest woman, so I figured I'd jump right into the pit with the boys. I weighed about 115 lbs at 5'8" but always made it through somehow. At that weight, I probably just bounced like a pinball through the chaos and out the other side.

When I started college in 1991, the Riot Grrrl message had spread to the east. I had always considered myself a feminist, so I agreed with so many of the principals, but it wasn't 100% me either. Regardless, I just kept discovering more about what resonated as true for me.

It's pretty known by now that the Epoxies was my first band. I felt like an observer up to that point. I absorbed information. I watched people. I was so shy that I said little. When I ran into Jesse (FM Static), who I had met in college, at a party, and he told me about the new band he was working on, I asked if I could try singing. It was a request made specifically to scare the shit out of myself, but the whole thing ended up much larger than that.

I can truly say that joining that band changed not only the course of my life, but the course of myself. When we started touring and I was meeting strangers who knew me only as a voice or a person on stage, I realized that an interaction was my

real first impression. People liked what the band was doing; people liked what I put out there. I was grateful and humbled. Just because I might be elevated anywhere from a half foot to six feet on a stage doesn't make me any better than anyone else. That's silly.

Regardless, any of us might be energized by someone we see perform. Somehow a person becomes this slightly otherworldly thing to observe rather than interact with. I find psychology and sociology fascinating, so I was very conscious about trying to be accessible, kind, and compassionate. On the other side of the coin, I was (and

JUAN'S B-DAY BASH/ BURNSIDE BOWL BENEFIT

EPOXIES

Minds

buttfrenchers

AND THE HEARTATTACKS

RAFFLE!
PRIZES!
SPONSERED BY:

adidas
cbr
MY FATHER'S PLACE
SAVIER

$6
9PM
ALL AGES
NOCTURNAL
1800 E. BURNSIDE
SAT. JULY 26TH

am) just as grateful to anyone who takes a moment to tell me that they are inspired by what I do. It inspires me right back.

I haven't done music since 2009, but that's when life surprised the hell out of me—all my footholds disappeared and I was left with myself, family, and some supportive friends. That's plenty when it comes down to it, but I was faced with a complete rebuilding of my life from the bottom up. I didn't have a place to live. I didn't have a job. I know very well that I might not have made it through without my touring experience or a deep DIY mindset.

This time period is in the top three most difficult times of my life, but through that fucking pain, I knew I could face it *because* of all I had learned. Yeah, I started with only a bag of concrete mix (an analogy, of course), but a lot has come since that time.

In 2012, I had many basics back in place, but I decided to go back to school and take a break from music. I didn't know it at that time, but that led to my current enrollment in one of the best MBA programs in the country. This past August, I ripped up 20 years of roots in Portland, OR and relocated back to Massachusetts. This would be another in my top three hardest things I've ever done.

Masters of Business Administration. How unpunk is that?

If I was aiming to get into finance for the sake of finance, I'd agree with you. Hear me out though.

While I was in the Epoxies, I was reminded that I like analyzing numbers and learned that I find business to be pretty interesting; however, "business" is often a turn off to those with artistic leanings. Business is often, understandably, viewed as rich exploiting the poor for financial gains. We see this as the case more often than ever these days. But, within these norms, there are new approaches to traditional business taking place. These ideas or companies are often called social enterprise or B-corporations. These companies can be for profit or non-profit, but consciously make sure that the company's commercial strategies work toward improvements in social and environmental well-being (for employees of the company AND society) alongside profits for shareholders. This approach is also referred to as the triple bottom line.

I am a firm believer that knowledge is a weapon, and sometimes a stealth weapon. I also believe that this knowledge does not have to come from a formal institution. We are at a time where we can be curious about almost anything and learn through an amazing amount of free resources. I am a huge fan of *khanacademy.org* and the fact that MIT has the course material for their past classes available online for free.

Jawbox with Kim Coletta

Kim Coletta shaped the equilibrium for Washington D.C.'s godfathers of angular, jazz-inflected, post-hardcore punk Jawbox, who always put integrity above profit while making albums that sound wide-open one minute and restrained the next. Like others of their ilk (Shudder to Think, etc.) they took the guardrails off punk and brought wholesale change to the genre, igniting a third wave of Dischord, the iconic record label. Instead of anger coursing through their veins (like Minor Threat, SOA, Void) or harnessing left-wing leaning sympathies (Scream, Soulside), they chose an underlying sense of pure poetics while still remaining firmly in the humanitarian camp.

Whereas late era Government Issue (featuring Jawbox front man J. Robbins) yanked a few elements from classic punkers the Damned and projected robust rock'n'roll back into the D.C. soundscape, Jawbox shifted gears towards more abstract and stylized sound structures that left listeners both enthralled and vexed. Between their well-honed, seminal albums *For Your Own Special Heart* and *Jawbox*, Robbins charged ahead by writing lyrics that felt like Bob Dylan's leftover notes from Tarantula; in addition, with Coletta seemingly hyper-caffeinated behind her hard-driving bass, they paid endless homage to a cultural sea of influences, from Joy Division, Big Boys, and the Avengers to Frank Sinatra and Tori Amos.

Their power was evident from the first self-titled single, especially on tracks like the incessant, ready-steady-go "Tools and Chrome." On the earlier works, featuring hard-pounder Adam Wade behind the drum kit, the band nurtured their post-Government Issue modern rock with punk gestalt, meaning the music is squarely within a more trad-rock camp ("Consolidation Prize," "Manatee Bound" "Grip") with strong hints of earnestness, flawless delivery, and conspicuous smartness. Coletta's bass playing thunders to the surface most prominently on tracks like the infectious, slightly low-key "Spit-Bite," the slower, tuneful, harmony-laced rev-up "Channel 3," and the lashing "Tracking." The latter administers dueling guitars with grinding efficiency and hardiness.

Then *For Your Own Special Sweetheart* inaugurated the era of drummer Zachary Barocas, which re-shuffled and rejuvenated the whole sonic imprint, one blistering track after another, starting with the barn burner "FF=66," in which Coletta's bass threads through the chaos like a soldier criss crossing a minefield. The music is a basin of snapping drums, harrowing off-kilter guitars creating a lacework of noise, and honey-vocals turned sour shrieks. "Savory" became their modest "hit," flanked by Coletta's insistent stop-start bass, borderline ephemeral rhythm guitars, crunchy lead blasts, and the soothing cool vocals of Robbins.

Released just a few years later, their portent last, self-titled album features even more mind-bending, cornucopia drumming, from "Livid" onward to "Chinese Fork Tie" and "Won't Come Off," though they still remain capable of being surgically compact and able to unleash distilled magma on the "Mirrorful." The shepherded softer hues of "Iodine" also enrapture as the guitar lines helicopter to and fro. Yet immediately the next blistering track "His Only Trade" is a helter skelter affair full of bass foraging and dual-vocal narratives that seem to weave, smack, and sneak into each other, which creates an agitated, harrowing sequence no Pepsodent can ease.

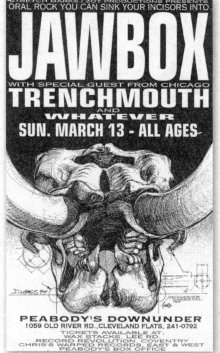

STRETCH MARKS / ZOT PRODUCTIONS PRESENTS
ORAL ROCK YOU CAN SINK YOUR INCISORS INTO

JAWBOX

WITH SPECIAL GUEST FROM CHICAGO
TRENCHMOUTH
AND
WHATEVER
SUN. MARCH 13 - ALL AGES-

PEABODY'S DOWNUNDER
1059 OLD RIVER RD., CLEVELAND FLATS, 241-0792
TICKETS AVAILABLE AT:
WAX STACKS, LEE RD.
RECORD REVOLUTION, COVENTRY
CHRIS'S WARPED RECORDS, EAST & WEST
PEABODY'S BOX OFFICE

Poster by Derek Hess

Jawbox never tapped the dead buttons of redux, tried to create a Xerox of some long-gone cruder time, or commuted to the corporate world, even while making records for a major label. Along the way, Coletta also forged DeSoto Records, helping boost the path of admired bands like Compound Red, The Dismemberment Plan, and Beauty Pill.

Kim Coletta

I grew up in Nashua, a small city in southern New Hampshire on the Massachusetts border. I was an odd combo of nerdy/jock-y/new-wavy—a variety pack that wasn't cool at all in a large, public high school in the mid-1980s. But we weirdoes found each other as they always do, and I moved away from Violent Femmes and embraced punk/hardcore in the sometimes-violent Boston music scene.

John Falls

My male friends at the time were all in bands, and I delighted in watching them practice and play shows. Sadly, it didn't dawn on me in high school that I could be doing that too. I chose my college partly because Washington D.C. got me a fair distance away from my boredom in Nashua, and I'd heard tales that D.C. had a great music scene.

After moving to W.D.C., I began to go out to shows, sometimes as often as three times a week. Unlike shows I went to in Boston at the time, there were more women at the shows and incredibly diverse bands. I was lucky enough to stumble onto Revolution Summer in 1985; a time of positive social change that railed (in part) against violence and sexism in the current music scene.

In my sophomore year at Georgetown, I bought my first bass from David Grubbs (Squirrelbait, Bastro, Gastr del Sol). For the next couple years, I played around with this bass while forging what would be lasting friendships with folks in the D.C. music

Kate Hoos, 2019

scene. After graduation, we formed Jawbox, and my music education began in earnest.

Our first drummer, Adam Wade, was a super rock drummer, and I learned a lot playing with him. But my bass playing took a different and positive turn when Zach Barocas joined the band in 1992. We were beat-centered (as opposed to timekeeping), syncopated, and unrelenting. We assumed that rhythmic parts could be as much hooks as harmonic or melodic ones; we saw the harmony in rhythm as J. and Bill saw harmony in melody.

I experienced some terrifically sexist moments early on such as a sound guy in Baltimore stupidly grinning and inquiring, "Do you know how to plug your bass in, little lady?" But I was fortunate to be part of a newly emerging indie rock world where more and more women were getting up there and kicking ass. I owe a debt of gratitude to women who came before me and hope I played some role in influencing those after.

The Dt's with Diana Young-Blanchard

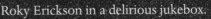

Best known for *Nice'N'Ruff Hard Soul Hits Volume I* (Get Hip), the band is sometimes more like a slow voodoo, monster mash molasses version of the BellRays and then next a breathless, motorcycle-greased 1960s/70s raspy icon Janis Joplin. These Washington purveyors of dirtyville volume borrow heavily from guitarist Dave Crider's haunted heritage as the meat-grinding guitarist of infamous Monomen (Blanchard was the back-up singer on their searing cut "See My Soul"). In turn, they soulfully shred songs ranging from John Fogerty to Roky Erickson in a delirious jukebox.

They released scorching vinyl on Gearhead and Estrus, even soaked up stardom in far-flung Basque country in Spain, where the rebel-hearted people seemed to long for an electric bastard blues that bridged retro Memphis soul music crunch with a modern heaviness measurable in buckets. For instance, no doubt John Fogerty knew that his

"Pagan Baby" was a shit-kicker, a sex-romp, and a plea for pleasure seeking sublime sin, but when the Dt's kick into full gear on it they unleash a hurricane of fried gator and wind-whipped southern gusto.

Meanwhile, as the wily chanteuse behind Madame X, Young-Blanchard produced retro-kicked gems like "Nobody Loves You Like Me," which pops like a 1957 A.M. radio rough cut gem, a Sputnik era blues warbler with brooding keyboard. She released a mini-album (10") and a single for Estrus Records, blurring the line between Billie Holiday and Holly Golightly: the work is earnest and ear-friendly, but if one doubts her ability to produce thunder, then clips of the Dt's on Spanish TV, like "Too Much Woman,"

prove much. She can unleash hard-shaking grooves and unbridled lung power like few others.

Diana Young-Blanchard

I have had so many influences. My introduction to music came pretty early. Even before first grade, I spent long hours devouring the 45s my father had accrued as a youth: Little Richard, Elvis, and the regular 1950s genre stuff was how I cut my teeth. In addition to this, I received exposure to groups like The Shocking Blue and all the best early country/pop singers and writers, like Waylon Jennings, Merle Haggard, etc. My first paying gigs happened during family gatherings where relatives would give me quarters for emulating Tiny Tim, Ethel Merman, and the voice of Snow White, for early on I discovered a talent for imitating through close study and practice.

During this era, I heard Etta James for the first time, and I remember distinctly deciding, "I want to sound like that!" I started seeking out music more purposely at this point and remember a period of female jazz and blues obsession, then Otis Redding, Wilson Picket, Al Green, all this before ever hearing the Rolling Stones, Led Zeppelin, or even Janis Joplin. Upon first discovery of Janis, I learned that it was possible for a little white girl to sing like a black girl, and after dicking around here and there, trying to get a band going with guitar guys I met in school, I joined up with some older biker dudes playing cover tunes in bars on the weekends, getting paid extra for "singing like Janis" for an audience of bikers in the late 1970s.

I spent too much time at too young of an age hanging out in bars; however, a spark was fanned that led me to continue through the years, including early punk/new wave bands in the 1980s (one of which I was the drummer). I played a shitty show in the warehouse of an apple orchard with the Screaming Trees once—one of their first shows ever. They were babies. Between then and now (fifteen years with The Dt's), I have performed jazz with piano accompaniment, sang with a mid-sized Latin/pop ensemble, and done some hokey country swing style music in addition to various other things.

The question, "What is it like to be a woman rocker in a male dominated world" sort of begs some kind of tale of discrimination. However, my initial response is that it's been pretty fucking awesome. I really haven't had anything but great experiences and positive acceptance. For sure, men dominate the rock world. It is mainly a sausage fest, but I usually feel like the lucky gal surrounded by an entourage of men who both commend and respect me for my ability to kick ass and deliver the goods. That's what it's all about.

I've never felt objectified or condescended to in any way. Certainly, there are one or two instances when some dude thought I was the girlfriend of one of the guys in the band or something, but I found this amusing and knew that following a Dt's performance, that guy was gonna feel like a schmuck.

Over the years, The Dt's has seen an increase in female fans, and I am thrilled when members of our women audience tell me how much of an influence I have on them, and how seeing a strong, confident woman rockin' hard on stage inspires them to wanna do it too! Now that Patti Bell is back in the band, I feel the "fairer" sex has an even stronger presence.

One negative I just thought of. Traditionally, most rock clubs do not cater well to ladies' toilet needs. On the road especially, it's hard to find a decent place to doll up before a show or take a crap. Overall, as stated by the great Jack Endino, friend and producer to The Dt's, I am "not the diva in this band."

Speaking of Jack, he has been fantastic to work with. We have recorded with him so many times over the years, and he is truly a Dt's fan. He knows and understands the sound we want and appreciates that we know what we want going in, so the process is symbiotic—a mutual musical endeavor. Jack actually plays an awesome and crazy guitar lead on an original tune coming out on a 10" around April of this year via Valley King Records. I have spent many vocal sessions, microphone positioned directly behind Jack and the mixing board, while the rest of the band is situated in the actual recording room in front of us, so we have become especially intimate in the recording process. Oftentimes he dances around the soundboard while I'm recording—it's so cute.

Sarge and the Reputation with Elizabeth Elmore

Somewhere between surging college rock (indeed, they stemmed from a Midwest college town), smart melodic indie rock urges, and soft-leaning (not exactly bubblegum) but also equally nuanced emo punk existed the bands of Elizabeth Elmore, including Sarge and the Reputation, who made bewitching companions to the era of Promise Ring, Jets to Brazil, and Texas is the Reason. With fluid dexterity, Elmore (alongside bassist Rachel Switzky) could deconstruct everyday relationships on "Beguiling" and faltering communication and disappointments on "Stall."

Tougher still on tunes like "Fast Girls," with its big sizzling guitar tones and wrangling rhythms, she could describe being enamored with punk rock girls, using a style that feels as compressed and intense as nimble rock'n'roll haiku. Meanwhile, "Dear Josie, Love Robyn" catapults with neo-hardcore beats. It layers Elmore's own sweet sounding—but actually imploding with vexing anger—vocals on top, like buttercream covering smoldering coals. "Detroit Star-Lite" takes aim at self-obsessed girls, the postcards we leave behind, and the souring price of ambition. It jolts with lean energy, limber drums, and effortless wordplay. More than a mere rocker, as a lawyer, she has also been keenly interested in Civil Rights, Child Welfare, Foster Care Issues, and musician-related territories, proving the conscience of punk runs well beyond power chords.

Here is an excerpt from an interview I published with her in my magazine *Left of the Dial*.

LOTD: You once said, "I think it's really weird to put a bunch of people on a show together just because they're girls. I can maybe understand ten years ago, people saying there is sexism in music. There's sexism in music now, in the alt and punk rock scene, but it's very subtle and very nuanced and it's not that women can't get shows anymore. Now it's become this girl ghetto and has become the last bastion of marginalization . . . So, then we are telling girls, or girls think that they need female role models, so then we have mostly sub-par female role models they are looking up to." Has the Reputation dealt with the same subtle and nuanced sexism or . . . has the girl ghetto been liberated, or have the walls become just more invisible to the naked eyte?

Elmore: I don't think the girl ghetto can be "liberated" in the sense of some heroes flying down to set all the poor girls free—mostly because the gender-focus is largely self-imposed and frequently created, validated, and celebrated by women as a form of empowerment. I don't happen to view it that way (though I love the fact that Lilith Fair was conceived of as a way for women artists to show their collective economic strength. That's rad.) What I don't understand, as I mentioned in the *Punk Planet* article quoted above, is why gender needs to be an issue at all. I'm generally pretty offended when I realize we've been booked onto a bill with bands we sound nothing like and have nothing in common with simply because the bands contain women. I think it's patronizing, marginalizing and most importantly, really reductionist of women as musicians. The music we play, what we sound like, and what we believe in seems to hold no weight with certain booking agents—we're all girls, so group us together. It's annoying and condescending.

Yes, women are sometimes treated differently, but I think there's a pretty broad spectrum depending on the individual women at issue. We're talking about musicians here and if someone's getting the job done, they'll be respected. And there are women who complain that they're being treated differently when honestly, they're just *not*

David Ensminger

holding their own. More than anything, I notice women are perceived differently in the first place—there's a presumption, due sometimes to the fact that many women in the music community seem to be content to be sort of silent girlfriends/participators or adulating groupies, that we're there to be supporters of the community, not playas. I see it all the time and it sucks and it's not fair.

But I guess my main disagreement with the stereotypical feminist view in rock is how a level playing field can best be accomplished. I think women accomplish a lot more by walking the walk than by theorizing and philosophizing about how best to accomplish the walk or pointing fingers at people they believe are preventing them from making the walk. Women are frequently dismissed as musicians because audiences have seen a lot of women who have not made the effort to learn how to play their instrument well and seem to think they have no obligation to (well, that, and sometimes guys are just moronic assholes. But that's sort of a given).

Due to a sort of misguided P.C. effort, I think clubs or shows run by men tend to give women shows before they're ready so that they can make some sort of declaration about how progressive and liberal they are—that *they're* not part of the problem— without ever having to examine the ways in which they *are* part of the problem. And then the people with entrenched views about how women can't hold their own are given one more piece of evidence supporting their beliefs.

The Warmers and The Evens with Amy Farina

The Warmers convey the same incisive intelligent design as Alec MacKaye's triumphant, art punk leaning Ignition, on display on Warmers' cuts like the halting "Red Light Runner" and the breathless, surging "Berretta U.S.A." Behind it all is the mercurial drum work of Amy Furina, always plowing towards open forms, not quiet in her pursuit of rhythmic furor.

The Warmer's smart, challenging, unhesitatingly exploratory eponymous 1996 album is an essential post-hardcore document, starting with the sizzling, shivering "Snake Charmer," but the entire album produced a web of recalcitrant songs that stay in the bloodstream. If Fugazi expanded their musical palette as they matured, The Warmers blueprint from the beginning seemed to defy convention, to avoid rock as usual, but not to lose themselves in a rabbit hole of math rock either. Even when they are on tenterhooks, restlessly inventive, they aren't overly ponderous.

The Warpers at Cynthia Connolly's opening reception for "People from DC in bands with their Cats" at GO! Cd in Arlington, VA. 6-7-1995, 1995 Cynthia Connolly.

With tunes akin to Circus Lupus and Faraquet colliding with Gang of Four, they dissect the nature of rhetoric ("Mad at the Man"), or plans to avoid people ("IWAAY"), in which Farina's drums career in jazz-like flourishes and pure unshackled damaged funk-rock. The closest they come to playing it "straight" is during moments of "The Lowdown," which quickly give way to hectic moments of loose stomp, riffing, and declarations. For Jawbox-style luster and heightened, skillful interplay, note Farina's winding fills, as well as elastic timing, on "No One Like Me No One Like Me," which compliments the overall abstract poetics. She is equally unleashed and mesmerizing on "Walking Solves It." If any band in D.C. came close to Sleater Kinney, this is it.

The Evens, featuring Ian MacKaye (brother of Alec) and Farina, less is proven more. As a co-singing duo, they produce muted appeal within reserved tendencies. They replace the emotional cliff-hangers and dissonant dexterity of Fugazi with domicile (un)rock; they once toured by Greyhound bus, include house lamps on their gig stages. The nasally MacKaye maintains a kitchen sink style, wielding unfussy rhythmic thrusts that dance with Farina's incessant, propulsive grooves and her stark voice.

Cadences found in the mesmerizing "King of Kings" unfurl at the speed of Lungfish and reveal wry wordplay and alliteration. Meanwhile, "Wanted Criminals" approximates an avid social critique, decrying an age of hive-mind shadow surveillance, while "Warble Factor—Version" and "Let's Get Well" mine the existential tension between nature and fakery—media concoctions of beauty and finance. Recalling Samuel Becket's endlessly re-worked language, the band shows listeners that intelligence is not measured by social media spin and hype but by exploring roads less traveled...

Psych-Punk Freakout: An Interview with Ariane Root and Tara McMunn of The Ultra 5

T hough most punks endlessly rehash memories of New York City hardcore and crust, the frenetic all-ages gigs at CBGB and ABC No Rio, or the burgeoning straight-edge scene, a whole other underground music scene existed in the debauched margins—lurid, primal, fuzz-toned, and feral. This scene was awash in retro clothing and addicted to hunting down dust-clogged 45's and spinning organ-drenched, head-spinning sonic platters at loft parties and dark cluttered clubs, some on the fabled West Side.

The Ultra 5 stepped into that intense subculture rife and overflowing with fetishes. Partly shaped by the swagger of the Cramps and the Stooges as well as the vintage aesthetics of Count Five, 13th Floor Elevators, and ? and the Mysterians, and much like their counterparts the Vipers and Fleshtones, they honed a raw psychedelic pastiche, but with one vital difference: two women, Ariane Root and Tara McMunn, formed the rhythmic backbone.

Ariane, you just didn't create colorful artwork for your own band . . .

Ariane: I worked as a designer at *Star Hits* starting around 1986, and then as an art director for *Metallix* until about 1992, when they fired me for a black Skid Row cover. I guess it didn't "pop" off the newsstand, but what can I say, the color black was a statement in those days! Both magazines were from publisher Felix Dennis of *Maxim* fame, who was quite a character. But the *Metallix* years were fun fun fun, lots of stars and musicians coming through the small office on 39th street.

I guess the Xerox was the computer of the day. We spent a lot of time working with it to create the mechanicals for layouts—moving and stretching type, creating distressed textures. Also, we used a lot of black ink to make splotches and create bloody type, which we Xeroxed and cut up. At some point, like the early 1990s, the color Xerox became available/affordable, so that's why I think the color collages/posters that I made for my band's (The Ultra 5) gig flyers became a new option.

Tara, did you help with the visuals for the records and flyers?

Tara: No, it was all Ariane. We had our own graphic artist, so no need for my help there.

In many ways, Ariane, you seem like a product of the Midwest: a serious hands-on work ethic, a dedication to the notion of rock'n'roll as being a kind of force of life, an attention to details and history . . . Do you see yourself as a Kent art student at heart, or not?

Ariane: You are really a product of where you come from and what you learned early on. I took piano lessons, which gave me the skills to play keyboard and bass in bands, and I was always making things because I couldn't afford or find the things I wanted in Ohio, so a future in art and music is the only thing I thought would really work!

When people think of rock'n'roll, they forget about Ohio as home to Devo, Pere Ubu, Dead Boys . . . or where Bowie first hit it big on America radio. Ariane, were you aware of that cultural zeitgeist even before going to college?

Ariane: Yes, Cleveland rocked. We grew up with Ghoulardi (Ernie Anderson) on TV and heard a lot of new music on radio station WMMS. Cleveland was a testing ground for record companies to try out new acts, so all the bands came through there. From huge World Series of Rock concerts at the stadium to Robert Gordon and the Plasmatics at the Agora. Bands like the Cramps, X, the Damned, and local bands like the Pony Boys played at clubs in the Flats or on the west side. In college, at JB's in Kent or the Bank in nearby Akron, I saw great bands like Pere Ubu, various iterations of the Dead Boys, Rubber City Rebels, Hammer Damage, the Action, Wombats, Generators, F Models, Ragged Bags, Unit 5, Human Switchboard, Chi Pig, and The Bettys.

How did other women in music influence the both of you—Tara, you were in an all-girl band, right?

Tara: I grew up in awe of cool rocker chicks like the Runaways. I wanted to *be* them. What's cooler than a leathered-out, sexy girl with attitude and a guitar? I was inspired by Poison Ivy and the Cramps, Blondie, Courtney Love, Vixen, Nina Hagen, and Lena Lovich. Punk rock will always be my favorite, but I went through a big ska phase—The Body Snatchers were the shit! There was the 80s hair band metal phase. Staten Island had some top-notch all-girl metal bands that would blow away the boys! Misdemeanor, Wench, and Brat—these metal chicks were dynamic, a force to be reckoned with.

My girl band, The Maneaters, only lasted about two years in the mid-late 1980s, but it was the funnest two years of my life. We were enormously popular in N.Y.C., played all the cool clubs, opened for the Chesterfield Kings at Irving Plaza, played in Boston a couple of times, and took part in an all-girl tour of Canada. These gals were seriously bad-ass, getting into bar brawls, getting arrested, ingesting psychedelic substances

Tara in Zero Child with author, in NYC, 1997

(oh, the stories!), but just remarkably talented! The Maneaters were Shari Mirajnick on vocals, Andrea Kusten Matthews on guitar, Luda Lutz (RIP) on guitar, Ellen O'Neil (RIP) on drums, and later Piki Soul a.k.a. Piki Houde on drums.

Ariane: My favorite bands were the ones *with* women in the Cleveland/Kent/Akron scene. Guitarist and keyboard player Susan Schmidt and bass player Deborah Smith of Chi Pig, Tracy Thomas the singer and synth player of Unit 5, Myrna from the Human Switchboard, the all-girl performance art band the Bettys, and of course I was influenced by others like the Runaways, the Slits, Siouxsie, Chrissie Hynde, Deborah Harry, Exene Cervenka, Kim Gordon, Candy Del Mar, and Poison Ivy.

Ariane, what drew you to New York City?

Ariane: I was in my last semester at Kent State, and they asked if anyone wanted a paying internship in New York that was starting in two weeks. I raised my hand and said, "I'll be there!" I must have somehow known how limited my prospects as an artist would have been in recession era Cleveland, and NYC sounded like just the ticket out.

Tara, when we first met, you lived on Staten Island—have you spent your whole life there, and has that given you a different perspective of NYC life and music?

Tara: I was lucky enough to grow up here in Staten Island, right across the water from NYC, and quick access to cool venues like the Peppermint Lounge, The Ritz, CBGBs, Danceteria. For a while, we would go to the city every weekend to see whatever band was new and exciting. But we had lots of cool bands come to play right on the island at The Paramount. In the 1980s, My boyfriend at the time was deejaying at The Paramount, so I was lucky enough to see and even meet so many epic 80s bands. Too many to list here, but to name a few, PIL, The Dead Kennedys, Anti-Nowhere League, Bow Wow Wow, Squeeze, The Plasmatics, The Specials, Wall of Voodoo.

When I think about the garage rock scene of the city, I imagine the Cramps, Fleshtones, stores/mail-orders like Midnight Records, Venus Records on St. Marks, used clothing stores in the East Village, etc. But how would you describe that scene?

Ariane: After living with some friends on St. Marks Place when I first arrived, singer/guitarist Bob Urh moved to NY from Ohio too and we found an apartment in Chelsea. Midnight Records and The Dive were nearby. The Dive was a bar where we started hanging out in the 1980s garage rock scene. We saw bands like the Fuzztones, Fleshtones, A-Bones, Maneaters, Optic Nerve. It was a scene of mushroom haircuts and 60s biker movie attire, with the most fuzzed out sounds I ever heard. Bob picked me up a Vox Continental organ, and we started The Ultra 5.

Tara: Looking back at that garage scene, the days of The Dive, I'd say, I feel so lucky to have been a part of it. To those that never experienced it, I'd say it was like being in a groovy 1960s movie. Everyone was dressed in hip-huggers and paisley with

mysterious dark sunglasses, the girls with mini skirts and gogo boots, the guys with mop-style, bowl-cut hairdos. The music was fuzzy and trippy, with swirling organ and vintage in-your-face fuzz guitar. The parties were outrageous, with people tripping and dancing like they were in a Beach Blanket Bingo movie.

Tara, Vox organ seems like the uber-instrument for garage rock, but how did you imagine your role in the band—did you study licks from classic garage bands?

Tara: I never studied licks from classic garage bands. I just played what I felt. It probably wouldn't have been a bad idea to study some of those licks, but my basslines were inspired by whatever I was feeling at the moment, and, of course, whatever the drummer was playing.

Unlike a lot of punks and hardcore kids, who were naive, amateur, restless kids working in basements and with cheap nearby Xerox machines, Ariane, you studied design and worked for metal fanzines, where you dealt with bosses and customers/fans, all while making your own surreal Dada-meets-meets Monty Python gig flyers. What was navigating between the two different worlds like?

Ariane: NYC was pretty much like the movie *Taxi Driver* when I arrived in the early 80s. We were starving artists I guess, living on a slice of St. Marks pizza a day, in ratty six-floor walk ups but just so excited to be in NYC, free and creative. The magazine work didn't pay well but did allow for the rock lifestyle. I remember showing up to work on two hours sleep or in my clothes from the gig the night before. There were other musicians who worked there, and the editors were always out partying with the bands, so it was somehow sort of tolerated.

Of course, we all looked at the punk graphics coming from England, and the Dadaist were the reactionaries of their time, so they were a big influence. The Swiss International Style of graphic design was what they were teaching when I was in college, using sans serif typefaces, asymmetrical layouts, and stark b&w photography. But I didn't really learn much in design school. Living and working in NYC was my school of hard knocks.

Ariane, you mention the stars coming through the office up at the 39th St. office— when you saw that side of the business, did it reveal much to you, not just about the rockers, but the whole idea of rock'n'roll as product? Did you want the same for The Ultra 5, or something different?

Ariane: Those years definitely opened our eyes to the possibilities of what we could achieve with the band in contrast to our earlier pure art rock. I myself liked having a creative outlet as opposed to "corporate oppressed" design or music. We could do whatever we wanted with the band, and we were rebelling against our daily grinds, which was necessary to survive in NYC, and, in turn, allowed us to be creative.

Tara, do you remember your vision of the Ultra 5—did you want to be like the Cramps or Fleshtones, something contagious and distinct within punk culture?

Tara: Well I didn't think too much about what I wanted people to envision us as, at first. But then I started to realize that what set the Ultra 5 apart from the others was that we were not just slow and creepy, but slower and creepier than the others, darker, murkier and swampier than the other garage bands. I realized one day that this sort of spooky, eerie, ghoulish thing we had going on was what the fans were drawn to. It spoke to a very specific primal thirst.

Tara, didn't you work for Musician—so how did that provide a look at the business and dynamics of mainstream music?

Tara: Oh, no (laughs), somehow that appeared on my Facebook page, and I'm not sure how. I think when I first started my Facebook page, it asked what I did for a living and I didn't want to mention my boring office job, so I said musician.

Many people are surprised to discover how many women worked in the nudie mag business, from designers and photographers to business clerks, etc. Were

there many women staffers at Metallix, or were you a rare presence, and what was it like being a woman in the business?

Ariane: Yes, there were several women where I worked, but it was a real boys club. Especially since our publisher came from the 1960-70s British rock publishing world. But I just found those oppressive ideas about women in rock or in business really outdated, and didn't let it stop me in any way.

So little has been written about women in garage rock, whereas much has been focused on, say, Siouxsie and the Banshees, or Riot Grrrl. Do you think women have been left out of the storytelling, and not just the rockers, but the photographers, designers, etc?

Ariane: I don't think anyone really thought about who was behind a poster or record cover, that someone had to make it by hand. Designers were invisible, behind the scenes. Now that everyone uses a computer, I think there is a better understanding of how things are created, and more of an appreciation of the graphic arts and women in arts.

When my band first went to play in Mexico in the early 90s, they had never seen any women in rock bands, and a female reporter interviewed the bass player Tara and I about it, saying things like, "In Mexico, women would be viewed as 'Putas' or loose women if they played in bands." We were like, "Errr, no, in the U.S. there are women in bands, and we grew up understanding that women could do or be whatever we wanted."

And when we first played in Mexico, there weren't any women in the audience, only guys. But that all changed a few years after we first played there, and women were even starting bands! I like to think we had something to do with it.

Tara: Well, we found out for sure that the Mexican women were indeed influenced by Ariane Root and I when the Ultra 5 played in Mexico. One day Bob Urh was walking down Second Avenue by a record store and saw an album in the window that had similar artwork to the Ultra 5's *Dead or Live* album. He went in the store and picked up the album and saw that the band was an all-female band called The Ultrasonicas, and they were from Mexico City. He contacted them and asked if they had heard of the Ultra 5. Their response was, "Heard of you?! We named our band after you and The Sonics, our two favorite bands!" We were just blown away. Then we heard their album, and it was just amazing, the epitome of cool garage music by insanely talented women. If you haven't heard The Ultrasonicas, this is an essential to any garage music collector.

Tara, how would you explain the band's appeal in places like Greece and Mexico?

Tara: Well we were completely taken by surprise by the response from the Mexican people when we played down there. I would have to say that I believe Mexico City had the largest population in the world at the time we went to play there, and the DJ that brought us down there played our record on the radio, where something like 20 million or 30 million people could possibly tune in. You didn't have whatever regulations and red tape you had here in the states that would prevent a band like us from having our record played on commercial radio.

So, there was nothing stopping this not-overly popular New York band from being heard by the masses. The response was just astounding! The fans were wildly enthusiastic. I remember one night after a sound check, we got in the car to go

back to the hotel to change for the show and there were crowds of fans just pawing at the car windows like we were the Beatles or something. It was surreal, like a dream. We came home with suitcases full of gifts from so many really wonderful fans. They made us feel like rock stars the three years we toured there, with each year an even greater response than the year before.

MYDOLLS

First festering in the musical mélange of 1978, when the death of disco was imminent and the 'blank generation' sought a second life, Mydolls became the South's ambassadors of artful, anarchic, antsy, and angular sonic territory. From AK-47 and Bevatron to Legionaire's Disease and Derailers, women permeated the underground. Mydolls, though, has remained predominantly female, with the lone hold-out of drummer George Reyes, the cousin of singer/guitarist Trish Herrera. Their family had deep roots in Latin music, which rubs off on Mydolls' quirky Latin syncopation and uprooting of punk standardization. In fact, their tune "Breaking the Rules" lays that groundwork.

Borrowing tendencies from No Wave, darkwave, Mancunians like the Fall (whose "Totally Wired" they resurrect with glee), Siouxsie Sioux, the Raincoats, and 'year zero' punk while forging their own brand of genre-free meanderings, Mydolls have shape-shifted on nearly every song by pursuing ever-changing musical forms; the poetry, in turn, comes quick, fast, and full of dramatic vocal enunciations, political vibes, and allusions.

Their cerebral know-how and mischief-making is plentiful, including making tons of collaged flyers for gigs, being the subject of endless haunting photography, and even unveiling their own brand of spoken word endeavors. All of it proves their boundless capacity to shrink down and merge the world of music and fine art. Sometimes their

imagery winks savagely: "I gave my niece a punk doll: when you stick her with a safety pin she screams and says, 'Fuck! Fuck! Fuck!' The doll is nice too," announces one flyer in handwritten script, while another juxtaposes a newspaper blurb about gun control with the clipped out headline "Coping With Sexual Pressure."

Locally, in Houston, from working at iconic clubs like Paradise Island/Rock Island/ The Island to being knowledgeable staff at Real Records (operated by U-Ron of Really Red) and Vinal Edge or even owning Rat Records in Rice Village, women have proved their worth behind the scenes even as others found limelight in the hazy glare of stages and smoldering clubs. Linda Younger of Mydolls likens the eruption of her own band, as she told me, to "a perfect storm . . . . We were friends with several great Houston and Austin punk bands who supported us completely and kind of adopted us as their sister band, inviting us to open for them and even go on tour with them. There was social unrest and frustration. We wanted a way to express that angst by writing our own lyrics and music, not performing cover versions of what others wrote. The result was music that was not the typical punk rock of the day. The title of our EP describes our approach: *Speak Softly and Carry a Big Stick*."

Mydolls carved tunes that seem spectral and poetic ("A World of Her Own" "Walls of Tunisia"), reeling with punk combativeness ("Exorcism" and "Christmas Day"), and bursting with jazz skronk ("Apology"). Others are molded with an influx of festering drums and modulated bass akin to early New Order ("Imposter"), stiffened post-punk rigor ("Rape of a Culture"), soft starbursts ("Please No Mary"), Pere Ubu-like musical manifestations shot though with feminist decrees ("In Technicolor"), and nervy mutant surf well within the radius of B-52s ("Nova Grows Up").

After releasing seminal recordings on CIA Records (alongside bands like Really Red and Culturcide), appearing on BBC radio in Britain with legendary DJ John Peel, touring the East Coast from Pittsburgh to NYC, and appearing in *Paris, TX* by German director Wim Wenders, which won the Palme d'Or at the 1984 Cannes Film Festival, they disappeared into the black hole of history. Over the last decade, though, they have emerged from their mythic underground status to resurrect their unique style and gain new notoriety.

Gigging frequently (including a summer 2016 stopover at the illustrious Contemporary Arts Museum in Houston that hosted a temporary retrospective of their gig and record art), revisiting their catalog, and forging fresh tunes that feel as ambitious, harrowing, and unhinged as ever, they released the 2017 album *It's Too Hot For Revolution*, and were inducted into the Houston Music Hall Of Fame.

Linda Younger

As I sat down to write this, my heart and head swam with all the musical memories from my past. It was like stepping into a time machine that transformed me into the little girl from Lafayette, LA, whose daddy was the band leader in a 16-piece big band called Charlie Aillet and the Skyliners. Everyone loved Charlie for his incredible ability to make them feel special and loved his wonderful sense of humor. He played at lounges in Lafayette and had a weekly television program much like Lawrence Welk or Doc Severinsen. My sister and I appeared on it once to sing "Let the Sunshine In." It gave me that little taste of performing in front of an audience that planted the seed for what was to come. I played his saxophone in the Furies, my high school band. He taught me "Tequila," "the Swim," and the

"House of the Rising Sun," and those were the only three songs we played (laughs). I still have his saxophone now, one of my cherished possessions. I can never repay him for all that he taught me about music and life. For me growing up in Lafayette, music was all about Motown, James Brown, Lightnin' Hopkins, the "Harlem Shuffle," and Mardi Gras. Of course, there was Woodstock and the Vietnam War: those events definitely expanded my little world tremendously. Then came the Beatles, the Kinks, the Rolling Stones, and so many other new influences. Music was again one of the most important ways I had to communicate, and I listened to it nonstop.

I moved to Houston in 1973. Until then, I really didn't pay attention to punk . . . that soon changed when I met Ronnie Bond (U-Ron Bondage), who introduced me to punk rock music and Trish Herrera. Rock Island/The Island was our hangout, and Real Records was our connection to so much new music and an awakening due to the empowerment inherent in listening to, dancing to, and eventually playing, that music.

Mydolls started in 1978 at Wavelength Hair Salon as part of my new haircut . . . my bangs initiation. It seems strange to say, but there was something about that haircut and the conversation with Trish and Dianna that happened that day that enabled me to see things much more clearly. It was like we were on a mission to tell our story and step up where women had not traditionally been before. Writing our own music, and in so doing getting such enormous satisfaction from having others relate to and enjoy it, was infectious. My musical influences at that time were the Raincoats, Slits, X-Ray Spex, Patti Smith, Siouxsie and the Banshees, the Cramps, the Velvet Underground, and Nico, among others. Doors opened, and so did we, playing with Siouxsie and the Cramps in the early 1980s at clubs like Numbers. Then we decided to tour the Midwest and East Coast, from Kent to New York City, and take a trip across the pond [Atlantic], where we met John Peel. This journey to explore and experience life continues to this day.

As I reflect on all those years, and what it means to me to have found punk rock, I think it was the realization that what you felt and what you embraced was important to share . . . Also, not being afraid to be different, and to stand up for what you think is right regardless of what others thought about it, matters too. And that gave me the ability to find others who felt the same and were also not afraid to put it all out there and see what happens.

Women in Punk are definitely a force to be reckoned with, and we are not going away. Now, go make a band!

FRIGHTWIG

Clear & Distinct Ideas Presents

D.O.A.

SeaHags · *Frightwig*

FRIDAY, APRIL 24

CLUB CAN'T TELL
1227 K STREET, SACRAMENTO

Advance Tickets At:
All Ages · Information: (916) 444-3133 · All Ages

Frightwig continue to exist as a raw, delirious, and disorderly counterpoint to all that is stiff, staid, and formula-driven about punk. In doing so, they unleash reckless, sizzling entanglements with art, fury, and fun, all while injecting a muscular feminism that bows to no blowhard creed or single truth. Before the artfully acerbic shock rock antics of Riot Grrrl and the rock'n'roll gender subversion of L7 and Tribe 8 came the behemoth noisemakers Frightwig, whose line-up convolutions (more than 12 members past and present) match their unbridled sludge-meets-acid punk wall of sound that marries the world of Chrome, Flipper, and Bomb with bash'n'pummel feminism, wacky street theatre, and tuneful chaos.

In 2013, they self-released *Hit Return,* showcasing them both then and now, like the veteran shredded disco onslaught "A Man's Gotta Do What a Man's Gotta Do," (1984) which was right at home with their former tour mates DOA's version of "War" and "The Midnight Special." The gals load it with bombastic horns, bump and

grind bass, psychedelic-discharged guitars, skittering hi-hat dance floor drums, and skewering wordplay. That slab is joined by the straight-forward flare gun of "Crazy World" (1986). Increasing the tempo and pace, they also unfurled "Big Bang" from the same delirious album. With snarling talk-cum-prose vocals and whirling guitar/keyboard interplay hinting at off-kilter Velvet Underground traits, the bulldozing tune feels like a barbed wire jukebox hit that takes the exoskeleton of Joan Jett and Patti Smith and fills them with hot molten lead. Instead of pop pomp and poetic epiphanies, they pen blood-curdling vignettes for the dank and dreary, pissed and unforgiving.

Claude Shade, 2014

Though the tune "Crawford" does carry its weight well and contains all the sly sonic kernels of vintage Frightwig, I have to admit the caterwauling vocal attack of "My Crotch Does Not Say Go," (1984) with its propulsive, cave stomp percussion and determination to present both female fury and cutting insight, does feel every bit as atavistic as the day the band peeled back post-hardcore's possibilities. Though they might have erupted from the same period as the Pandoras, who featured Kim Shattuck, and Screamin' Sirens, led by punk icon Pleasant Gehman, they feel like sisters from another more blood-boiling planet.

Mia d'Bruzzi

I came to San Francisco as a 16-year old punk in 1980 and was lucky to immediately fall in with an amazing group of artists and musicians who were busy changing the world through subversion and misbehavior. Some of the movers and shakers of the time were the Mutants, the Dead Kennedys, Flipper, the Offs, the Lewd, Bad Posture, 3 Day Stubble, Tragic Mulatto, Factrix, Tuxedomoon, to name only a few; also adding to the fervor were the budding performance artist Karen Finley, *Creep*, *Search & Destroy*, and countless other 'zines that artists and punks xeroxed and put out themselves. I felt right at home and commenced upon smashing the status quo in any way I could. The earliest organized form of this was a band called G.O.D. (stood for Girls on Drugs, Girls Overdrawn, or whatever we decided according to our mood that day). This early all-female outcry then gave way to the birth of Frightwig, sometime in the fall of 1982.

Deanna Mitchell and I found our collective voice one winter while on unemployment, drinking and raising an unholy racket in my warehouse. Once we were joined by Cecilia Kuhn on drums, it all came together as a feisty hairball of female fury and fun. We were on a mission to challenge the pervasive misogyny of our times. We *never* felt like victims, however, and were, and remain to this day man-lovers, not man-haters. In those days, what we were doing was unusual, and quite offensive to some, and I think that we gained many opportunities as a result. Our first proper tour was supporting the Butthole Surfers across the east coast, and it was fantastic fun playing in NYC at Danceteria, the Pyramid, and the 8BC in the East Village summer of 1984 was a time I'll never forget. I had left college to tour, and I didn't make it back to school for many years!

Cat Farm Faboo was recorded at Hyde St. Studios in 48 hours. It was truly a case of throwing massive handfuls of sonic spaghetti at the wall and letting the producers

sort it out. Phillip "Snakefinger" Lithman (RIP . . . he worked with the Residents) produced it along with Bruno deSmartass (Bad Posture, Sluglords, Flipper) and Garry Creiman (who also engineered). I really wished I had tuned more carefully and more often . . . We brought all our friends in to sing back-ups, and it was completely bonkers. It's certainly not the most musically accomplished album, but we really meant what we said, and I figure that's what matters most.

I left Frightwig in 1986, pregnant and searching for a good spot to nest. I ended up in Honolulu, where my daughter was born in June 1986. I returned to S.F. with her in 1989 and joined the legendary Mudwimin. We ended up putting out several singles, two full length albums, and touring the U.S. and Europe over the following six years. Frightwig reformed in 1995 and did a short stint in Europe as well. I also played in several other bands during this time, but I'm pretty sure you haven't heard of them. I got clean and sober in 1997 and went back to university in 1998. In 1999, I went on an exchange program to study Industrial Design in the U.K. While there, I started a band called the Juicy Bits, which won the Battle of the Bands (surreal experience— there was nowhere else to play—it was in a semi-rural area!). I played with Fabulous Disaster on their first European tour in 2000. While in the UK, I met another guitar player on my course at university, and we partnered up. We both graduated in 2001 and returned to S.F. to live. Neither of us works in Industrial Design, but we have had several bands together, have recorded a bunch of albums, have a record label called Ptchoo Productions, and have an 11-year old son (who shreds on guitar like you would not believe!).

I have been making a living busking for the past six years. In order to do this, I play *a lot*! I mostly play at Farmers' Markets and outdoor events, although I still do shows at clubs and restaurants. I play originals as well as covers, but I make more money playing songs people know. I also sing jazz standards and have played a quite believable show for the S.F. Chamber of Commerce Gala Awards Ceremony—they had no idea I was really a crusty old punk rocker! I have mentored a kid's rock band called Sticky Situation for the past three years. We've recorded an EP and an LP for them, and they write the *best* songs. They continue to amaze me with their talent and creativity. I currently play in the following projects: Mama Mia d'Bruzzi & the Spicy Meatballs (originals); Dizzy Twin (studio recording project, new album in 2017); Connie Champagne & the Sparkling Wynettes (Tammy Wynette cover band); The Mutants (back-up singer); and of course, Frightwig. Music has been my salvation and I am deeply grateful to engage in its creation every single day.

Zipperneck/$50.00 Goat with Mel Hell/Melissa Waters

Rock'n'roll history is mired in the trials and tribulations of self-abuse, including tales about potent, intelligent, and savvy musicians taking the highway to hell. Yet too often the other side of the equation goes unnoticed. For some, rock'n'roll offers a recurring salvation, recovery, and coping mechanism, a way to face down and even triumph over adversities and ailments. For bands like Mydolls, whose members have struggled with alcoholism

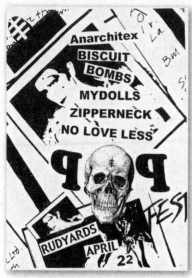

cancer, to Alejandro Escovedo (formerly of the Nuns with Jennifer Miro) coping with hepatitis-C, music provides a sense of community, healing, and empowerment: hence, it becomes a powerful way to navigate life's travails.

Melissa Bransfield Waters is known affectionately by local Houston tattooed tribes as Mel Hell, the high priestess of Joan Jett-style music. As decade-long singer and bass player for Zipperneck and longtime underground punk icon, she has appeared on the cover of the *Houston Press* and been featured in three lengthy profiles. She now performs in $50.00 Goat, advocates for people suffering from Trigeminal Neuralgia (from which she also suffers), and is a Board Certified Behavior Analyst that works with children and adults in need.

For ten years she and sidekick Jerry McDaniel consistently unleashed dizzying rock'n'punk in their well-honed band Zipperneck, who fervently covered Oi classics from Sham 69 ("I Don't Wanna") as well as Midwesterner fare from the Zero Boys ("Civilization's Dying") as much as penning their own guitar-heavy, bravo music. For Waters, music has become one of the only forms of solace and mental health maintenance in an otherwise tumultuous recovery from a routine dentist office visit gone terribly awry, one that devastated her health and personal life.

In April 2011, with a tooth hurting due to a cavity, she headed to her local dentist, who administered a lower jaw block—a Novocain shot on the right side—to prep the filling. Yet, in the air-conditioned placidity of the office, she suffered Trigeminal Neuralgia.

"I felt several electric shocks travel throughout the injection site and out my tongue. She said, 'Oops, sorry. I must have hit a nerve.' A week later I still felt no feeling in the right side of my face and had frequent shocks in my jaw, lips, and tongue."

This was not just a sore swollen gum: the discomfort indicated something much more serious. "I was drooling and spitting while trying to talk during meetings at work all week. I even played a show in severe pain and spit all over the audience."

Returning to the same office, the dentist proceeded to diagnose a root canal on the same tooth. Instead of being concerned by the intensity and frequency of pain, the dental assistant chimed in, "Sometimes this happens . . . everything should return to normal in about 8-12 weeks . . . try Sensodyne toothpaste." The office offered no prescription, no sage advice, no hollowed medical formulas. They just suggested a tube from a drug store usually meant for people with dentin sensitivity and receding gums.

Her condition quickly worsened. Upon seeing an endodontist, Mel hoped for a final solution. The doctor's own nonchalant response, though, varied very little than previous assessments. "I asked if it was a good idea to inject the same area while it was still all wonky, and he said, 'Yes.' I trusted him because he's a doctor. I asked for laughing gas because I'm scared to death. Then he asked what genre of music I wanted in order to drown out the drilling sounds."

Waters chose the bombastic comfort of Classic Rock, a blast from the past to alleviate her anxiety. "The chair went back, Skynrd's "Free Bird" started playing, the gas mask went over my nose and mouth, and I was a happy girl. So, he slipped in the shot . . . "

"I screamed and grabbed his leg. He said, "Oh my God. I'm so sorry. Did I hit it again?"

"'Uh huh'" . . . is all I could say since my mouth is propped open like something out of a Marilyn Manson video. Tears streamed down my cheeks. The only thing that kept me calm and still was hearing 'Jukebox Hero' and 'Crazy Train.' I flashed back to [being] a 4-year-old tow-headed little squirt, riding around Oak Forest with my mom in her red Chevette."

That dream and sense of peace were cruelly short-lived.

The Mayo Clinic, well-respected purveyors of medical insight and usually clinically cautious in its descriptions, defines Trigeminal Nerve Pain as "one of the most painful sensations *in human experience* . . . excruciating." As they note, it damages sleep patterns, overall health and well-being,

and employment prospects. Most worrisome, the condition can commonly lead to suicide.

"The worst part of this disorder is the aftermath of an attack," Waters admits. "I wake up drenched in sweat, groggy, sore, and alone. It's a terrible feeling to realize you just lost another entire day of your life. A day that could've been spent with your friends and family, or helping others, or playing a gig.

"The deafening silence and isolation of the empty apartment . . . is more terrifying than anything I know. I wonder if this is why my Great Granny Haynes flipped the switch on her stereo the minute she woke up and then kept it on until she fell asleep at night. Music makes you laugh, dance, and sing. It helps you to forget all your troubles and remember you are not alone."

Currently, she sings with the $50.00 Goat, a jet-fueled and limber unit that wrestles with tunes ranging from the Damned to AC/DC. Despite her years of undiluted pain, she continues to be a crucible of whiplash soul-punk, a mouthpiece for all that is true and righteous about rock'n'roll, and a top-notch veteran.

For some, music is simply innocuous aural wallpaper, a leisurely diversion. For Waters, music is a lifeline, a way for her to keep afloat as the world bears down, heavy burdens and all.

Melissa Waters

I got my first zit when I was 11. Up until this point, I had floated along with Top 40 music, setting my taste on cruise control from 93Q on Monday mornings, clear through until "Casey" Kasem's long distance dedications on Sunday afternoons. But now there was a blemish: a subtle yet poignant prophecy of the turbulence to come as I dipped my feet into the deep end of human development, otherwise known as adolescence.

To say there were ups and downs during my teenage years is an understatement. While I had big plans of being on the varsity cheerleader squad and becoming homecoming queen, a hormonal hurricane ravaged my sweet angel face, as well as my mind. By my early teens, I knew I had to find somewhere to hide, and quick. I scanned the Jersey Village High School cafeteria daily for a safe place to dine. I was in search of people who didn't care that I looked like Robert Smith from the Cure (I had to use so much concealer to cover up my acne that I could have passed for a mime).

Then, one day I found an empty seat at the table closest to the band hall. I was drawn to this particular location, because, unlike the cookie-cutter haircuts and clothes that littered the majority of the mess hall, this table was chock full of leather motorcycle jackets, homemade safety pinned T-shirts, and hair that defied gravity. Hell, one girl even wore a wig. These were the punks, and they loved me for who I was. I was surrounded by Rico from End Result and Chris and Mike from the Dreggs (who later became Slaphappy). I did get to go to homecoming after all, but with my dude friend Eddie, who smiled politely at my parents as we took pictures, then secretly whisked me away to Fitzgerald's for my first real "show." It was 7 Seconds.

The show at Fitzgerald's broke the seal. I was indoctrinated into all things punk, oi, and otherwise 1-2-3-4. I regularly snuck out of the house to go see the Hates. When I wasn't at a show, I was holed up in my bedroom listening to KTRU, recording my new favorite bands (Minor Threat, Ramones, Sex Pistols, GBH, Exploited, Dead Kennedys, just to name a few), and circling all of the band T-shirts I wanted to buy out of my Burning Airlines catalog.

Much to everyone's surprise, I survived into young adulthood, went to college, and started a career in Special Education. I picked up a bass guitar somewhere in my mid-twenties, after being told by a very annoyed boyfriend that I needed a hobby. It was a good thing I listened to him because that hobby later became my lifeline during the tougher sides of motherhood, divorce, and catastrophic injury. It never once occurred to me that women couldn't be punk. In fact, how could we not be?

PROFILES

Something Fierce with Niki Sevven (Niki Williamson)

Something Fierce's DIY release *There Are No Answers*, which was picked up by uber-garage punk label Dirtnap Records, offered up blurry, hectic punk insistency that left listeners pogoing somewhere between the heyday of 1977 (The Lurkers, The Boys, etc.) and 1997 (The Queers and Pansy Division). But it also packed plenty of searing Texas-based melodic punk (Marked Men, Riverboat Gamblers). Together, it all created testy and tense, smartly mustered, handwrought pop and punk, especially on the likes of "Teenage Ruins."

Singer Steven Babyface Garcia sweats and yelps in volcanic volumes, bassist Niki Sevven (former member of the punk pied pipers of pandemonium Vivian Pikkles and the Sweetheart Uber Alles, as well) hits the bass with finger-bleeding venom, while shaggy drummer Andrew "Red Rocket" Keith has arms like a Mustang's legs in action. They make bubblegum-tethered, shack-shaking mayhem that radiates, not nudges.

Balancing sincere teenage alienatiotn ("Aliens") and note-for-note re-imagining of Buzzcocks and company ("Passion is A Fashion"), they plumb the past without melting into mishmash mimicry. Dynamiting their way through slight Stiff Little Fingers echoes ("On Your Own"), their lyrics examine youth and independence, while the harmony-laced "Where You Goin Man" and "There Are No Answers" sound hitsville-bound at 45 RPM. They seduce listeners with steady treading, keep-it-short, 45 vinyl classicism. *Don't Be Cruel* displayed a change of heart: they hand-pick post-punk elements to splice into the usual ripped and collaged punk mix.

TOYS THAT KILL
KEVIN SECONDS   KEPI GHOULIE
(7 SECONDS)   (GROOVIE GHOULIES)
SOMETHING FIERCE

HALLOWEEN 2012
AT WALTERS 1120 NAYLOR ST.
DOORS AT 8PM / ALL AGES / $8
$5 WITH A COSTUME

"Afghani Sands," for instance, feels less like "Fast Cars" era Buzzcocks and more like Magazine, mid-period Clash, and Alternative TV. The tune's energy rises to the surface with a scratched glassy surface sheen. Thin insolent guitars, a terrifically thick serpentine bass, laid-back drums, and trembling vocals range close to artful effervescence.

Sevven's thermal, throbbing bass gives tracks like "Don't Be So Cruel" plenty of heat and dance floor saturation as the fidgety guitars and nonchalant drums broadcast a much different, dusted-off kind of punk mechanics that don't plough and furrow with noisy insistency but instead rove on the surface with textures and cunning wordplay. The intro to "What We Need Now" seems borrowed from the Only Ones, but the rest of the track feels like The Records, while "When You Hurt" seems as close-shaven and lean as The Undertones' heartful emotives and spry motorboating speed. And the funk-punk jitters of "Future Punks" is delectable, something at home on *Sandinista*, the Clash opus. Gone may be Something Fierce's honed abrasion and dire discord (like the sing-along tumult on "On Your Own"), but a new saucy dimensionality replaces the hard tracks. Bustling grooves champion over cutthroat rock'n'roll.

Their split record with Occult Detective Club echoes sound systems even older: the internal sense of time on "The Sound on the Northside of Town" is a gyroscope tilting back to the 1960s: fluffed vocals and raspy guitars form the two and a half minute tune. Meanwhile, the bass pulsing "Get On or Get Off," which stretches out to four minutes, is full of trance-like repetitions ("there's never enough") that flood the guitar rock tram-line. Never glued down or circumscribed by small-world punk circuitry, or eclipsed by mannerisms and burdensome nods to modern trends, the band crashed the gates of Houston punk and never looked back.

Milemarker with Roby Newton and Monika Bukowska

As the millennium unfolded, emo had taken shelter in pop modes, math rock unleashed charmless vanities, and street punk often felt sulking and rodent, but Milemarker felt like an expedition transmitting new frequencies. Their searing coterie of tunes, like "Signal Froze" (with its warped vocals, undulating electro vibes, and crackling rock'n'roll urgency) and dramatic "Shrink To Fit" signify their crack postmodernism.

Monika Bukowska, Milemarker, by David Ensminger

Roby Newton, Milemarker, by David Ensminger

Instead of mustering play-by-numbers angst, thin protest, and soon-faded disaffection—the stuff of teenage war cries—the music of Milemarker seems fermented in a nuanced analysis of the sensory-overladen landscape of late-capitalism and the information economy. Plus, they always feel shaped by prescient literary sources: William Burroughs, William Gibson, J.G. Ballard, and more. Hence, nothing in their music, lyrics, or composition is overtly stripped-down or bareboned. They offer no simple recitation of revolt. Instead, they approach tunes in a cyber-fiction way, creating scenarios, news dispatches, and memos from the digital edge, producing music that morphs and transcends.

Roby Newton's moody chromium voice fills tunes like the hypnotic "Food For Worms." She excavates all the damage done to women in a world of dead, damaged, suicidal heroines and forced silence, when the best minds of a generation starve for their place in intellectual and cultural spaces: "The girl's heroes have taken their own lives. We're left with sewn lips and model lines. The place for us: we are seen and not heard." She urges people not to take shelter in desultory destruction; instead, turn off the ovens, throw out the stones, shut off the gas, and don't enact the tragedies all over again. The song amounts to a call to liberate women from the dire ends of Sylvia Plath and others, to crush monocles of madness, and to fight omnipresent confinement, barriers, and censure.

Yet, despite heady preoccupations, Milemarker can still unleash pummeling power and slanted rhythms, like "Sex Jam One: Sexual Machinery" and the holographic punk of "Tundra," which doesn't feel a million miles from Kanye West (as does their urban dance-throttled "Idle Hands"): it gnaws on incandescent keyboard riffs, the drums explode in sudden urges (from jazz-bridged syncopated asides to sheer fist-stomping smackdowns), and the slow, degraded guitar forms a distorted sonic plumage. Newton and crew weigh in on the impending ice age by using the song as a stretching harsh light to illuminate the impending eco-cataclysm, which will upset economies, military agendas, populace routines, etc.

Having taken a break since 2005, they have re-emerged, like nomads populated with new band members and up-to-the-minute visions. In Europe now, with Monika Bukowska providing the unflinching keyboard roil and rhythm, they heave up songs like "Conditional Love," an electro-punk motif frosted with sing-along punk propellants. It's dancefloor-odored and ordered, an electrifying emblem of punk hybridity.

The Cramps with Poison Ivy (Kristy Marlana Wallace)

While some franchised psychobilly can seem like brooding, mumbling, overly-greased, flashbulb-postured hot rod anthems, the Cramps were truly mad as a hatter, more Screamin' Jay Hawkins than Johnny Cash. They offer a peephole into all that is bleak, weird, pitch-dark, eccentric, and trembling in the crumbling daguerreotypes of horror rock. Their exquisite "Human Fly" has garnered over 11.5 million listens on Spotify alone, so despite the band symbolizing a supposed primitive crudeness, they still intoxicate a worldwide cult following.

Lux Interior and Poison Ivy, the epitome of Teenagers from Outer Space/Incredibly Strange Creatures, represent the lunatic

fringe of the genre. They bring to life mondo garage, go-go music that bashes out the windows of normality and good taste. They were never by-the-book; instead, they acted like demented, leprous rockers with squalid beats whose "The Way I Walk" acts as a calling card, just as "Garbage Man" showcases the unholy mixture ("One half hillbilly / and one half punk"). No one else on the planet could allude to Pablo Picasso, black Chevy Impalas, Magneto, Comte de Lautréamont, Dr. Jekyll and Mr. Hyde, Marcel Duchamp, and cuckoo birds, just as they did on the album *Flamejob*. In doing so, they masqueraded as matinee-minded misfits, deviants, and gorehounds that actually were some of the sharpest kids in the paint-flaking, creaky, midnight mansion of punk. Plus, they lit candles on the path for Southern Culture on the Skids, Demolition Doll Rods, and Flat Duo Jets.

For four sizzling decades, despite any and all trends, they staggered back to the cave stomp of 1950s radio and TV inspired by the hyper "rap-rhyme mania and krazy" lingo of Cleveland horror host Peter Myers, referenced on their opus "Mad Daddy." Indebted to an era when powerful personalities allowed all hell to break loose on the dial/channels, the Cramps opened the door to punk's alleycat screech and howls. At a time when rock'n'roll had become the epitome of respectability—soft-peddled assured professionalism à la Styx, Toto, and Chicago—the Cramps were permanently primordial, with "Zombie Dance," "I Was A Teenage Werewolf," and "TV Set" in their earliest phases. All were full of animal noises, prurience, bizarre chants, wild-eyed vocalism, putrid psychedelia, and droning squawls. Later, they stirred up white heat, thumping big beats, and ever-hallucinatory riffraff like "The Creature from the Black Leather Lagoon," "Two Headed Sex Change," and "Alligator Stomp."

Lux Interior and Poison Ivy forever challenge the severe conformity of ingrained body-hate, perceived tact, and socially observed decorum often felt even within punk codes. They blew these all to bits, and the music—their mongrel rockabilly odes to shrieks, geeks, and freaks—remains eternally unchallenged. No other has come close in spirit, spasm, or strange fun. And Ivy was the muse that kept the idiosyncrasy in check, artfully, with a deep mystique worthy of endless flattery and fan worship.

The Saints with Janine Hall

Australia was always a sieve of booming punk dreamers. Yet Janine Hall is a figure obscure to most people, a pokeweed in the landscape of popular culture, an unremembered slice of the epic. Her contributions date back to the original warehouse days of punk reckoning and extend throughout the feisty 1980s. First, she provided the bass depth, craft, and ductile licks for the Young Charlatans, a band as much influenced by punk's condensed energies as it was by the ideas of composers John Cage and Bela Bartok. The band was partly affixed to the orbit of Trash, a clothing shop in Melbourne that outfitted the boys and gals of counterculture, and Tiger Lounge, where they gigged in 1978.

Hall's modulated bass introduces the turnpike-of-tunefulness, guitar-pop of "In the Mirror," a curious slab of light-rollicking that serves up a premonition of war, sudden loss, and ghosts in mirrors and window panes. It becomes a compressed saga, replete with intelligent parlance telling of blanked-out lives. "Don't let them take it away," Bailey announces, with alarm tempered by pop song structures in the vein of Nick Lowe, despite the annihilation dreamscape. But even better is their rough, subterranean tackling of "Dizzy Miss Lizzy," a ratty-armed embrace of R&B black musical antecedents. Beginning with an extended gurgle, it captures both the rough mien of the 1957 tune by Larry Williams (popularized by the Beatles, among others)

and is, by far, the most breathless, spine-plunging, dance-erupting track on the album, a true punk archeological stew of barroom brouhaha. Not unlike the Replacements on a bender, it is a cut that should have been a hit for a label like Chiswick.

Hall went on to play with the more mainstream Weddings Parties Anything, but her 1970-1980s punk musical signature, play-worthy and dispatched with talent and nerve in a time of narcissistic male overload, should not be unloved and or neglected.

Sado-Nation with Leesa Anderson and Mish Bondage

B ondage's punk tenure burgeoned first during the late 1970s, when Portland became an epicenter for moody punk that attracted touring bands like the Bags and Dils to venture up the coast. With a handful of diehard local women, she formed The Braphsmears, the first all-female punk band in the dark, dank, gray-hardened city. But by 1982 she joined David Corboy's already-lionized Sado-Nation, replacing Leesa Anderson (who debuted on their self-titled 7" on Trap Records in 1980). He had been a mainstay since the 1960s, an art student and guitar slinger featured in bands like the Avengers and Road Runners. By 1978, the punk bug hit him hard, and his rock'n'roll camouflage mutated into zenith punk tunes that shook the underground. Together with Bondage, the two forged an unparalleled mixed-sex dynamism rare in the hardcore era.

They don't explore teenage sores; instead, they explore the husked nerves of adults careening through a dystopian world. Their repertoire consisted of inconsolable rage, cutting and cunning observation, and unsettling, full-speed ahead riffage. In the beginning, they offered silos full of rancorous, gritty rock'n'pop cuts (Corboy on "I'm Trouble," Anderson on the intrepid "Phobias," Bondage on the superb "Cut Off the Cord") and later a barrage of hardcore, like the title track "We're Not Equal," a combustible barrage of blunted rhythms.

Mish Bondage, Sado-Nation

Bondage was an emblem of female strength amid malevolent boy-thronged, rattlesnake slam-pit clamoring. Never restrained or tongue-tied, never a softened little lamb of obeyance, and propelled by impatience with rock'n'roll's typical flat politics of partying, her rampant intelligence shone bright; she used words to clutch both prickly inner-anger as well as ideology ("Politics and Passion") as the band's beats riveted with the precision of a clock rapping to and fro in a steely surge. Above all, the lyrics aspired towards

the condition of freedom and dignity, despite the odds. Long before Black Lives Matter seeded a movement based on deep-held convictions about police's rampant harassment, mistreatment, and deadly profiling, bands like Sado-Nation appeared on *The Sound of Hollywood— Copulation*, an entire anti-police brutality compilation album on Mystic Records, where they delivered "Fear of Failure," one of their decisive, lightning-fast tunes that clocks in at one minute and tells some depressing truths ("hide behind a loaded gun / fear of failure"). d

Across their tunes, they were able to reveal dirt-smeared workshirt honesty that examined the dogged and downtrodden ("Ma and Pa Democracy" sung by Anderson, "On Whom They Beat" sung by Corboy) as well as scarred punk ideology examining the truth about a New World Order built via scaled-up violence, whether by police baton or SCUD missile.

Against the bleating sheep of conformity leaving many rapt with Reagan (the seemingly golden, unruffled actor with the wrinkled smile behind a fevered Republican surge), Sado-Nation calculated a sense of outrage, closely and plainly dicing up the woes of democracy in which dreams became burdens that had beset young America clawing its way out of doldrums and alienation—even as the dominant narrative was under the spell of videorama MTV and a New Romantic catalog of deodorized hits.

Bangs with Sarah Utter and Maggie Vail

Though capable of conjuring terrific tunes like the tough-skinned, visceral, garage-rock "Burnout" and "Maggie the Cat," Bangs' album *Sweet Revenge* was one of the strongest, pitch-perfect records from Kill Rock Stars, a chopping block of a label that had grown left-field, more geared towards a swathe of creatively crooked, experimental, wonky, and esoteric bands. Bangs were the polar opposite, offering a sweeping, vein-melting, mischievous slice of rock'n'roll with stripped-down, clandestine pop vibes as married to the first three well-worn albums of Cheap Trick (whose "Southern Girls" they occupy with confidence) and the legacy of Bomp Records (Weirdos, Iggy Pop, the Zeros) as it was to post-Riot Grrrl cinders, a genre Vail's sister Tobi helped ignite in Bikini Kill and her zine *Jigsaw*.

Tunes like "Docudrama" show a ubiquitous form of self-thrashing about how destructive patterns lead to a life unlived. It manifests a penal colony of one: the narrator is detached and marred by the feeling of "sensory overload" and anxiety that acts, metaphorically, like a clawing lion causing heart attacks due to sheer fear. Yet, those miserable conditions, and the subsequent psychology of such paralysis, are challenged by the song's sense of hope. The narrator, in a scrum of gathered nerves, begins to push aside the pain and amplifies a sense of rejuvenation ("I think I'm going to run / I think I'm going to try"). The music is turbulent, hot-headed, thumping with energy, and not at all bracketed by irony.

"Into You" waxes about desire ("put my lips on a space ship / and rocket to you") with banging, plugged-in, anthemic gusto that feels just one part removed from the sinewy crunch of Joan Jett or the Donnas. And their cover of Cheap Trick (also tackled by the Accelerators) is not a cross-pollinated rewiring of the original, not a stooped, patronizing, ham-fisted blunder: it's a wholehearted, organic, and clearly rendered embrace of the original. It is loaded with sweet air-bubble harmonies, easygoing pace, and a transfixing, plucked-heart pop sentimentality with a trebly sheen.

Colored by cynicism and disquiet, not the psyche of reverie but the urge of hard-nosed revenge, Bangs seem to offer a sequence of succinct, callused attacks against feeling down and out. They kick against the dead-end dance of a life gone wrong. Instead of placating someone's doldrums and offering mild circumspection, they offer dossiers of disgust, deliberately unfiltered.

Harmonically, they are pissed and ambivalent, consumingly volatile, but they facilitate a liberating catharsis in the process. Pain and break-ups are not mere glitches to be quarantined, they are part of the liquid flow of life. Do not shut out the light, don't exhaust your game, don't prohibit yourself, the Bangs say between the lines. Disentangle, smear the high-gloss retouched photos of fake life, and charge ahead because anger is an energy.

BANGS

The Rats, Dead Moon, and Pierced Arrows with Kathleen 'Toody' Conner

Few stories in the garage punk hemisphere can equal the partnership of military vet and Fred Meyer employee turned Portland counterculture Caffe Espresso owner Fred Cole and Kathleen "Toody" Conner, who worked at The Folk Singer. They met in the late 1960s when the Weeds, featuring the "White Stevie Wonder" Cole, were soon re-named as primal fuzz-charged The Lollipop Shoppe. The band ran out of gas in the drizzle-down former backwater hub of loggers, sailors, political dissenters, drop-outs, and beatnik bunkers like the Wayout and Café Orpheus. In this era, notorious stalwarts like Paul Revere and the Raiders and the Kingsmen drew much attention, and upcoming bands like the Mystics, U.S. Cadenza, and Notary Sojac made their marks. The musical marriage of Conner and Cole produced some of the most delirious, close-to-the-ground, gritty and poetic, intelligence-toting music of the last several dire decades.

Though the couple's musical legacy is a bending and nuanced tapestry, they are beloved mostly due to Dead Moon, their lo-fi rock'n'roll venture tinted with garage-folk, which ignited a dedicated following in Europe on the strength of albums like *Nervous Sooner Changes*. The band often featured the married duo dueting on tracks like "Running Out of Time." Their last unit before Cole died, Pierced Arrows, brandished harassing, mega-voltage riffage on tunes like "Guns of Thunder" and "Black Thunder."

But the couple's punk incubation, three self-released records released between 1979-1984, came to a full groan in The Rats. Though drummers fled them like melting ice, those works (alongside Neo Boys, Sado-Nation, and the Wipers) ushered in an era of Northwest punk that remains an ionized flow of greatness. They combined high art with tireless garage rock momentum and cool.

Starting with their self titled album, which unpacks "World War III" (not to be confused with the song of the same title by DOA), the band created a storage tank of tunes that focus on both the conundrums of a teenage domain as well as blazing issues of the Western world in crisis.

The beats on "Teenagers" seem akin to early Dils, slightly behind the beat, even awkwardly driven, like an updated Maureen Tucker (Velvet Underground), while the keyboard squirms of "Flash Dogs" shed light on the era when Cole opened for the Doors in his early band. It links to other like-minded tendencies by 1979/80 bands like DMZ/the Lyres (led by Jeff "Monoman" Connolly), but also nods to the Paul Revere and the Raiders' homegrown Portland kick seeking.

Though they seemed strangely reclusive to the rest of the world, the two remained a staple of Clackamas, Portland, their home for decades, where they continued to kindle their musical habits and run a business. Never second-rate, always stowaways on the edge of punk genres, always penetrating and carving a sense of cool when others stumbled, crawled, or succumbed to blandness, the two remained a tireless legion. With good taste and community-mindedness, they bridged a half-century of musical possibilities that the mainstream finds puzzling or degenerate.

Debora Iyall of Romeo Void

Before Beth Ditto of the Gossip challenged body shaming and gauntly thin body types present throughout much of punk and post-punk culture, Deborah Iyall was sending ripples through the indie music industry with her blend of poignant, feminist song cycles, epic singing, larger frame, and Native American identity.

She did not adhere to any readymade categories, just like her band Romeo Void, a multiracial outfit that debuted in 1979 in the thriving fulcrum of San Francisco, avoided easy classification. Surrounded by forerunners like the Nuns, Avengers, Mutants, Pearl Harbor and the Explosions, and more, they created an artful, empathetic, stylized outsider music that is melodious, chart-worthy (as in "A Girl in Trouble (Is A Temporary Thing)"), and smartly blended. As such, the band offered a tonic for punk hangovers and sounded more like discourse than discord.

Iyall, a member of the Cowlitz nation, grew up in Fresno and began her punk education by seeing the likes of Patti Smith. Iyall was an agitator at heart, having been part of the Indians of All Tribes takeover of former federal penitentiary Alcatraz that occurred from 1969-1971. As one of the more noticed Native American direct

romeo void

n v r   s a y   n v r
s a y   n v r   s a y
n v r   s a y   n v r
s a y   n v r   s a y
n v r   s a y   n v r

actions, like those of the American Indian Movement, it drew attention to treaty rights, land use, Bureau of Indian Affairs policies, genocide, and more.

By the late 70s, she immersed in Mabuhay Gardens, jump-started the Mummers and Poppers, a quirky punk-inspired band that rejuvenated 1960s nuggets, and thrived in the multilayered pedagogy shaping so many punks and artists at the San Francisco Art Institute. Meeting Frank Zincavage there paved the path towards Romeo Void's formation and endless gigs. Soon, they signed a deal with hyper-local music label 415 Records, who housed acts like SVT, the Units, and the Offs. None of them were by-the-book punks married to auto-destructive tunes.

Plaintive and restrained, but also narrative and tailored to observational, mournful, and mature truth telling, Iyall's grace, unapologetic presence, and stringently un-fragile nature are an ode to creative assertiveness in a time of facile pop platitudes. And as writer Denise Sullivan succinctly summarized Iyall's efforts then and now, she "uplifted and inspired, not only . . . brothers and sisters native to the Americas, but . . . fellow artists and anyone who's ever been broke or hungry, tired, or cast aside, and helped them to keep on keeping on."

Blackfire with Jeneda Benally

While many punk bands twiddle their thumbs and contemplate the entropy of Western Civilization, pose existential questions, or sort through pop culture flotsam and jetsam, Blackfire embodies the actual anti-colonial equation. Born from mixed Dine (Navajo) and Jewish heritage, this all-family three-piece, with Jeneda on bass, speaks to, and acts on, the issues that permanently seem to aggrieve and heavily impact Native Americans— despoiling and encroaching land use, endless genocide, damaged sovereignty, ongoing family and substance abuse, and much more. Despite the challenges of engaging two communities at once—indigenous and Western—they have sculpted both a remarkable music catalog and a tradition of bearing witness.

Their punk pedigree, unbeknownst to many, is the stuff that most bands dream of. They erupted from the Southwest with dynamic, well-oiled grooves and insistent protest music in the land of JFA and Sun City Girls, but few people have such special links to the Ramones, the godfathers of punk. Near his death, Joey contributed vocals to one of their trademark albums.

Native American Punk Rock
At the WOW Hall on 8th & Lincoln
Saturday, June 12th, at 7pm $5

Sister Jeneda—artist, dancer, model, spokeswoman for the Navajo Nation Tribal Employee Program and one of the founders of the Indigenous Youth Network, has become an integral part of community consciousness, as have her brothers. Such ethos was profoundly shaped by their father Jones Benally, a medicine man that occasionally joins them to perform as the Jones Benally Family, in which they honor traditional musical practices and their distinct heritage. They sometimes combine both with punk on gripping tunes, like the title song from their album "[Silence] is a Weapon," a churning, groove-oriented blast of protest rock. On tunes like the "It Ain't Over," Blackfire seed mid-paced rock'n'punk with volatility, heavy crunch, and meditations on the tragedy of compromising freedom in the name of security. Then the speed-soaked "Someone Else's Nightmare" features Jeneda joining her brother in the straining fray that recalls late-1980s hardcore, but with one musical difference and anomaly—a lulling melodic chant in the middle of the fervent barrage. The closest sonic kin might be Beefeater during their *House Burning Down* period. "Stand Strong" is an esteem builder, a call to pride, a way to split the dark clouds, find hope, and persevere against the odds, which have always been stacked unfairly against the self-preservation of Native Americans throughout centuries. The fight to protect sacred lands, again investigated by the international media since the Dakota pipeline spurred the coalition forces behind Standing Rock Resistance, compels people to hold together. Similarly, Covid-19's disastrous impact on the Four Corners region, which includes both Navajo and Hopi tribes as well as others, draws a spotlight on inequality suffered for far too long.

(Silence) Is A Weapon broadened their musical palate to include contributors like Cyril Neville, the funky percussionist/singer behind the Meters, without losing a sense of their swift musical volleys and inveterate conscience. "Common Ground" attempts to cut through class, color, creed, and genre. Jeneda's thriving bass complexity and pouring back-up vocals return to the fore on "Uprising," a pastiche of revolution rock, homegrown Dine glory, and mushrooming rhythmic variety. "How Can We Confess," however, is made from the same vertebrate of much 1990s punk, though they hungrily tackle the issues of gender, class, and sexual preference. Justice comes

to those who can afford it, Blackfire avers, as they encourage listeners to resist the "criminalization of dissent" and "stand against the fear and passivity."

Jeneda continues to plug away and tour with brother Clayson in Sihasin, which merges the world of drum'n'bass (not the genre, literally a two-piece unit) danceability with traditional music, also allowing her vocals to thrive in the forefront with the emotive, cunning, artful uniqueness of someone like Patti Smith (who herself channeled/appropriated Native spiritual music in "Ghost Dance," found on her 1978 platter *Easter*). Some people, though, might prefer Jeneda's tigerish performance on Blackfire's swift breathless cover of "I Believe in Miracles," one of the last seminal cuts by the Ramones. Likewise, she is a kind of miracle worker herself, joining Clayson in extended forays to Native American high schools, which too often suffer dropout rates and youth suicides twice the national average. They teach students how to mold songs, create hope, and find their voice. Truly, a punk act of conscience.

Circus Lupus with Arika Casebolt and Holy Rollers with Maria Jones

Holy Rollers first emerged by gigging at a Fugazi concert and became one of the bands that adamantly supported Positive Force commitments and actions that shook the nation's capital and aided the War Resisters' League/The Friends' Service Committee and Washington Peace Center, among others. The band's soaring, three-part harmonies and embrace of quirky rock, rather than heady post-hardcore formulas, encompassed multiple influences and made them stand apart.

Maria Jones was the beacon of the beat, the drummer behind their first albums, like *Fabuley*, which seemed to merge new shoegaze-y Brit-rock like Ride with Dischord bands including Rites of Spring on tunes like the surging "Changeling." It is a peon to strained personal relationships ("if you are open I will stay / rather than tearing us apart"). Plus, the tune features blunt stops and starts as well as a wild guitar ride and airy harmonies, which are overlaid like a soft blanket on the

INJUSTICE. WHAT CAN YOU DO?

Fugazi
Holy Rollers
Edsel

friday, march 24
8 pm

wilson center
15TH & IRVING, NW

info: 276-9768

positive force dc

Circus Lupus by Jen Semo

inner-chaos. Due to such salient tunes, they remain original and visionary, though at the time punks ignored them.

Other tunes like the slower output of "What You Said," with its interlaced harmonies woven atop each other, and its burning lyrics turning back to love again, seem like a 1960s pop quintet wearing bright shirts and unleashing crunchy guitars and earthquake rhythms. But "Skin Deep Guilt" not only features Jones' preeminent drumming—a kind of stunted, hectic funk drawing from luminaries like 1970s era O'jays and Funkadelic—but also go-go music in the tunes' midsection.

Instead of returning to the well-trampled fiber of Washington D.C. punk, they bumped against the paterfamilias. Like fellow labelmates Smart Like Crazy and Shudder to Think, they strayed down a novel path with new ingredients, producing curiously hyper-funky protest tunes like "We." They could pull in the slack and deliver exasperating speed, thrift, and then syncopated jazziness and spoken word on "Ode to Sabine County," featuring counterpart poet Julian Luecking. It describes a horrendous beating in an East Texas county jail: eight hours of unconsciousness, six children fatherless due to three racist officers. Like Bob Dylan's song "The Lonesome Death of Hattie Carroll," the song serves as newsprint and testament, a story of America's unscrupulous, hateful, vexing intolerance and injustice. Such tunes make Holy Rollers much more than mere inventive dabblers. They were workers of conscience, trying to upend both commonplace punk music scripts and a faltering legal system.

In the same era, Arika Casebolt served as the drummer behind Circus Lupus, led by cantankerous, inventive, and perilous-sounding Chris Thomson, formerly of Soulside. Though their stint was short-lived—a mere three years—they provided some of the most dizzying work ever to appear on Dischord. They offered up two albums of deconstructed punk and windshield-breaking anti-poetry whose spasms might have been foreshadowed by the Pop Group and Birthday Party. If in doubt, listen to the opener on *Super Genius*, the hallucinatory "Unrequited," a helix of twisted musical chops and radiation burn vocals. It's breathless, unlike anything the label had delivered.

By the release of *Solid Brass*, on which the drums are more muted by the engineer than their freshman outing, the band has gone off the rails. Their ever-mutating trajectories, on which they applied no hand brakes or coolant, became a bit difficult for some fans. Tunes like "I Always Thought You Were An Asshole" reek with Thomson's spurting, caustic, blood-curdling vocals wedged between brittle guitar pile-ups and relentless, changing drumming patterns. If Dischord music ever sounded more complicated and acerbic simultaneously, I do not know, though other tunes like the bluesy brawler "Takes About an Hour: Epilepsy" come close. Still, they do offer one tune that even casual listeners can lock onto—"Pressure Point." Though scorching, at least the tune feels approachable and even anthemic.

Like a photograph collaged and re-purposed for new art, they resurrect "We Are the One" by the Avengers, creating tortuously slow tumult from the original punk first wave's flicker of speed and fury. This time, though, they act as feral children, not the followers of Christ, fascism, or capitalism; instead, the ones that bury the past, they add lines to the frenzy, deploring wimpy folk singers, retrograde hippies, and "artist faggots." Not exactly the liberal fare expected from the D.C. circuit of the time, but part and parcel of Thomson's take-no-prisoners, heed-no-correctness approach.

The Groovie Ghoulies with Rochelle 'Roach' Sparman, Scampi, Wendy Powell, and more . . .

Plenty of hackneyed punk bands have plopped down a million miles of Ramones style surplus jingles, but only a chosen few cast their music with such earnest, flawless knack as the Queers, the Manges, and the Groovie Ghoulies—each execute the thrifty pop mechanisms, sift through pop culture debris, and exhibit heart-on-the-bubblegum-smeared-sleeves as much as the boys from Queens. For a quick taste, simply lock onto compact and pithy Ghoulies tunes like "Let's Do It Again," which bulldozes and bursts with memorable horsepower.

Like the Cramps used hiccupy, demented psychobilly, and the Misfits used dark crooning graphic punk (turned venal hardcore) to showcase a midnight mondo B-movie spectrum— zombies, human flies, martians, vampires, etc.—the Groovie Ghoulies do the same. They add, though, a surfy softcore slant, like "Chupacabras" (about the folklore creatures haunting the borderlands), "Deviltown" (about a town of vampire kids), and "The Beast With Five Hands" (mutant she-creature). All have one foot in 1950s A.M. radio bliss-out, when DJ Wolfman Jack over-stimulated an entire generation while oozing hip lingo and spinning slabs of knockabout vinyl. And instead of covering some common fare from the Ramones early catalog (say, *Rocket From Russia*), they scored a near-hit with their version of "Pet Cemetery," originally made for the Stephen King film of the same name, still a fave on satellite radio because it is utterly convincing.

For extended, classic cartoonish carnage, comb through their first-rate *Monster Club* album, which spares no loony subject: King Kong, the Blob, bats, the Lizard King, and 50,000 spaceships are just a handful of their narrative territories. Never drilling down too hard and severe in terms of their style, they keep things loose, but steaming. Thus, they effortlessly convert listeners to their whacky imagination

Bratmobile

Arriving on the scene like a raggedy power trio that remained proudly clattering, minimalist, and bratty, as well as fervidly smart, Bratmobile forged a threat to all that seemed over-produced, male-endowed, and pretentious. Though sending sonic communiques coded with underlined Riot Grrrl sensibilities, the band always felt more disruptive, duct-taped, disorderly, and disheveled than some peers, at least on their early shaky tracks like "Cool Schmool" from *Pottymouth*. It acts like an anti-brat pack ode in which the strident bass coils through the tune with more heavily-laden intensity, volume, and vigor than the drums and guitar.

EPs like "The Real Janelle" toughened-up their onslaught, like the tumbling, mow-down-the-poseurs, rancor-ridden "Brat Girl," which spares no spit, bile, and invectives ("get on your knees and suck my clit / if you are gonna lie and say that shit"). It is easily one of the most barbed slices of punk this side of early Plasmatics that makes much rock of the same period feel phony and counterfeit. Plus, on the EP Bratmobile reaches back to miscreant 1980s horror punk on "Where Eagles Dare" by the Misfits. The cut features Slim Moon of KRS Records yelping, and was labeled one of the "15 Great Misfits Covers" by *Rolling Stone*. In their hands, Bratmobile reverse-engineers the tune's raw and lo-fi ugly beauty. After Slayer and Metallica turned such horror rock fare to neutered stadium rock fodder, Bratmobile re-gifted punk audiences with the dark mess-heap of the rousing original.

By the time they forged tunes like "Flavor of the Month Club" (from *Ladies, Women, and Girls*) and "Shut Your Face" (from *Girls Get Busy*), the band had become impressive, multi-layered social commentators and more tamped-down players. The first investigates the leisure class conundrums of late-period capitalism, in which consumers are dizzied and overwhelmed by things. This foreshadowed the Internet era's rampant consumption ("You got your new clothes and your new friends to match / And too many dishes and a boyfriend, what a catch"). The irony is ladled thick as gravy, and the end game seems clear enough—the band seeks to subvert and pierce through the façade of a cellophane-wrapped life; hopefully, afterwards, something more real, authentic, and feminist can rise.

On the second album, they became woven-together, fiercely cogent players that decry the deaths of women and the unjust realities of male-dominated media even as they dollop the song with playful keyboards and surfy buoyancy: the effect is unique and disconcerting. Against the lite-punk grain, they inject a narrative about male cultural distortions, cover-ups, dismissals, indifference, and control. The band's outlook is global, too: they have a right to know, discuss, shed light on, and abhor the death of women, who are not invisible and silenced pieces of ass, anywhere, anytime. Though one's foot may be tapping to the bubblegum beat, the mind swims in the assertions and acrimony. Which is not to say they don't paint personal narratives of relationships in meltdown as well, like "Don't Ask Don't Tell."

Part and parcel of the Riot Grrrl insurgency, they also stand alone, with their own merit and ability, to show both the crisis inherent in the mundane, like dating, commerce, and being a youth. Plus, they probe larger, more troubling, and omnipresent anti-feminist superstructures. They don't unveil miles of sober didactics—they spot their enemies, adjust targets with wit, punchiness, and intellect, and still wrestle with enduring, uncomplicated rhythms easily at home on an Undertones or X-Ray Spex album. That is, they were not un-fun. They used the subterfuge of fun to ignite critical thinking. Scratch the surface. Feel their canniness.

The Interrupters with Aimee Allen

The Interrupters exhibit a wily embrace of punk-meets-ska heritage, from the unbound flexing of Selecter, the Specials, and Bad Manners to the no-nonsense, gruff, narrative pull of . . . *And Out Come the Wolves* era Rancid. To that brew, the Interrupters add a modern sensibility that is succinct, balanced between bravo street punk and two-tone. Even their clothing has flair—often they are bedecked in skinny ties and white button-ups. This mirrors their youth tribe danceable tunes perfect for South Bay underground culture.

Never sobbing, sullen, stricken, or stiff-lipped, singer Aimee Allen's roundabout path to the band started with a solo career circa 2002, stints writing with Unwritten Law, and appearances alongside Tim Armstrong. In Tim Timebomb and Friends, hear her on "This Time We Got It Right." Plus, she DJ'd on Indie 103.1 FM. She even wrote a tune for Libertarian presidential hopeful Ron Paul, whom she supported during his 2008 and 2012 campaigns. Then she cut two albums with the Interrupters, becoming a leading voice of accessible outsiderness—punk as tight-knit family values for talented and agitated drop-outs and renegades.

"By My Side" recalls the weight of personal history—growing up as "outcasts in a small town / in big sky country / in a pick-up truck with the music turned up." Against the grain of monotony, boredom, and stupidity, they survived with hearts-a-beating due to friendships that don't cave in when the streets become shaky. Friends are cadres—posses of like-minded, multicultural, beer-slinging, American Oi chanting hard-ribbers. These folks seem less poisoned by ideologies, instead bolting scraps of punk history into a matchbox of reverie, bonds, and underdog ethos.

"Take Back the Power" is their keep-it-brief protest anthem that doesn't stump for one party or another; instead, it sticks its middle finger into the nose of power and authority and encourages all the disaffected kids to find their power. Rather than cower and follow a lame liturgy of self-defeat, they urge people to possess the future and manufacture their own dissent against those agents who arrive in black suits, ready "to strip your rights away," a repression made possible by tax contributions propping up a supposedly "free" country. The judges and jurors don't favor those "who look like us," they avow, letting listeners understand the stark line between the haves and have-nots, the powerful and everyday people.

They don't just try to deprogram—they try to uplift, too, not by riding on the tail lights of Rancid, but fusing their hostile energies into profusely well-carved tunes that are as memory-inducing as a jolt of Operation Ivy. Plus, their catchiest tune, "She Got Arrested," bemoans the fate of women who fight back, using deadly firepower against abusers. They extol the sisterhood of avengers like most people extol football players.

Tex and the Horseheads with Texacala Jones

Just when critics imagined punk as a skinflint genre—tired, worn out, clichéd to the bone, and poor in imagination, cowpunk/roots punk erupted, creating new territories. Like it or not, Country/Western had always been tucked inside punk.

"Clean the Dirt," which featured Mike Martt and Jones crooning in a damaged duo rife with catastrophe ("remember when you caught my house on fire"), is boozy, colored by shades of restless, dark Nashville tunes (think of a grittier version of Jason and the Scorchers), and addresses the defects people bring to bear on relationships—the crud and crankiness, the psychosis and bare need. Jones, in her own idiosyncratic way, creates a sense that sex roles have shriveled and need to be shunted aside. "Baby, thought you'd realize / I got a pair of rovin' eyes / I like to be free to roam / and call anywhere my

home," she sings in her groaning, pumice-contoured voice that is impure, original, and otherworldly. By doing so, she stakes her claim to a world she can call her own. Meanwhile, the tempo is aggressive and the music is an earthy, raw cataclysm of molten guitar and lurching drums.

Never sedentary, Jones has continued, unabated as an unclogged stream, producing EPs that remain pregnant with power and luster, like *Fair*. Injected with an epidemic of urgency, it showcases some of her most aggressive tunes in years, like the fiery title track that careens like a Feeders or early Saccharine Trust tune. It conjoins abrasive, rogue surf with early 1980s swift tattered energy that blasts apart the monochrome 'woesy me' music of "alt country." The tune is seriously miscreant, fierce, and heart-pounding. The other tunes, "Dining with the Devil" and "Cousin It's Cousin," are equally bewitching and grassroots-inclined . . . They emit loosely ambling shambolic front porch weirdness.

Decades may fly by, the winds of time may curl back one's ears, one's hair may spot with piecemeal gray rays, but inventive, singular women like Jones don't grow old, quiet, and weary. They strike with newfangled determinism and backbone. It's not reinvention on her part, but a return to original fortitude and an offbeat sensorium. This produces music that is left-field, veering, bone-chilling, deadly honest, and never boxed-in.

Ruidosa Inmundicia and Accidente
with Carolina Demarchi and Blanca Rodya

With the fierce, deadly efficiency of bands like Dropdead (with whom they split a 7" in 2013), the Austrian band Ruidosa Inmundicia, led by South American singer Caro/Carolina Demarchi (who also plays dense, blistering guitar for Sotatila) from Chile, rips through the paltry reconstructions of hardcore punk with a blistering force all their own. Inspired by bands like Extrem and Gruftrosen (who also featured a female singer), the band flails against the detachment of everyday people who cannot see severe situations in front of them.

On the 7" EP *De Una VeZ*, which lasts a dizzying ten minutes, the band flips through tempo changes (similarly to the gymnastic musicianship of their *Huellas De Odio* EP), quick as mercury slipping, when not creating an impermeable wall of crust and noise. *Nunca Más* features haywire back-up vocals that recall the first few albums of raw power, before they became overt metalheads. Meanwhile, the scalding vocals and stripped-down sentiments ("Who are they / that lie with grace / and tell us / how we should proceed") fight the powers that encumber free thought. Musically, the lunatic speed and brash bravery, the menace and manifested pain, should cause anybody outside the punk subculture a panic attack.

But to catch a glimpse of their fermented power, their adrenalin-fuel, and their nausea and revolt against silence and submerged feelings, just watch them gigging in the streets of Barcelona on YouTube. The crowded Old World mise-en-scene becomes electrified—they contrast sun-scratched navels, corners with people hovering in fear, mild gestures in terraced yellow blocks, and festering decomposing dreams. The band adds acrid petrol to the crowd's fervor. In doing so, they flip an invisible ignition switch and use their music to ambush passivity and provide a bitter answer to the wistful tree branches of the public square and the frigid municipal landscape.

Accidente are a DIY enmeshed, Madrid, Spain, anarcho-punk band fronted by Blanca Rodya that contains all similar furor but skips harsh, screamo vocals and opts for a sweeter incinerator instead, though they sacrifice none of the speed and licks on their self-titled album. "*Vendiste tu yo al poder*" (roughly, "You Sold Yourself To Power") starts with a crashing siren, drum'n'guitar agitation, and then cruises forcefully, alight with the vocals of Blanca. Her tones remain melodic despite the insurgent, careening speed, which makes such tunes resoundingly anthemic and hummable rather than desolate and harsh. *Pulso*, from 2016, contains a more brazen studio presence spurting with heavy, unfurling, hook-laden guitars, driving vocals, and even more aggressive, triumphal punk'n'pop, like the title track, whose unpretentious lyrics speak some poetic truths: "*Dignidad no significó / que no grites cuanda duele / cuando hayas mordido el polvo / y tus demonios te superen*" (perhaps: "Dignity does not mean / that you do not shout when it hurts / and you bite the dust / when your demons overcome you"). The band is truly a surging, stirring combination of smart accessibility that is deeply underpinned with startling punk infusions. "*Escupe El Mar*" seems to combine both her ingrained, unquenchable sense of poetics and her sense of social justice. The narrative, which is rife with 2,000 bodies tumbling into the sea, seems to conjure the brutal failure of states to cope with immigrants—for these victims of borders and bureaucracies, the sea becomes a burial chamber that will never let them sleep. Their stories tumble in the manifold waves, like ghosts retelling the world their stories of horror and victimhood again and again.

Such traits—the weaving together of everyday experiences and pained nighttime memories, the large troubling nightmare of people desperately looking for new lives but finding only a waltz with death—combined with the band's instinctual, ferocious musicality—make Accidente a future-now band. Rodya neither shrugs away the moon or the haunting displays of inhumanity. Her ears are attuned both to the inner-frequencies and the murmur of the masses, not just the trembling tropes of punk.

The Goops, Trick Babys, and NY Loose

The 1990s witnessed the last remnants of mythic old New York beginning to disappear as real estate moguls carved up the city. Alphabet City touted by the Clash became just another gentrified zone. Chic and desirable pockets began to exist where squatters once dug-in (and C-Squat still occupies a building from 1872); the Poles and Puerto Ricans of Williamsburg were shunted aside for hipster bars and boutiques; the volatile, midnight squealing, jangled nerves of formerly riotous

Tompkins Square Park became a mostly calm oasis. Some sections remained immutable, like St. Mark's Place ringed with record stores (Kim's, Venus, St. Mark's Sounds), but soon that would change. As rock'n'punk began to grip New York City, a whole new legion of women arose that were far more heralded by the crew at *Flipside* in Los Angeles than their own brethren lurking in the boroughs.

They didn't fit with the scum and crust underground, or amid the fisticuffs-of-fury shaved head crews either, nor the downtown DIY spaces with the hardcore punk intelligentsia dispensing dictums of revolution. These female-led bands became a salient snapshot of inner city trash can rock'n'roll that flitted through the 1990s by forming their own criterion and consistency. The Goops, N.Y. Loose, and Trick Babys need to be restored to their rightful place in the punk survey.

The Goops, with singer Eleanor Whitledge, might seem like the closest kin to the co-existing hardcore milieu, since their gnarled "Barbed Wire Love" (by Stiff Little Fingers) debuted on the Blackout Records (which featured acts like Killing Time and Sheer Terror) compilation *Punk Rock Jukebox*. The label also released a handful of their singles and their self-titled album, though most 1990s youth know them due to *Mallrats*, which featured their slightly saccharine tune "Build Me Up, Buttercup." The

tune's video features suburban grunge hero Silent Bob (and Jay) showing how to stitch together a snappy video (like "show some idiot dancing"). Yet, the rest of the band's fare, like "Bored and White" belongs much more squarely with Joan Jett riffage. N.Y. Loose felt built from the same caliber of toughened punk as L7, though they cross-fertilized mid-1970s Alice Cooper with late-period Runaways, amalgamating a kind of taut, stubbed-out cigarette, lurid barroom bric-a-brac with a calculus for straight-ahead, uncomplicated lunges. "I wanna be your rock'n'roll," singer/guitarist Brijitte West booms on "Spit." That well-shot video features her writing on a couch, late-night Cinemax style, though her televised head replaces her persona on stage, like a displaced "cute face" torn from her actual body. "Bitch" seems to sniff at the rummage of Sylvain Sylvain (from New York Dolls) territory and rolls with the allegory of being disliked or chagrined for not being a self-loathing female, for not slouching and being glum in the face of everyday life. Similar sentiments re-animate on the hard-hitting "Detonator." "I'm so bored, but not as much as you are boring," West vents as she claims her space as a core-of-steel, clear-headed nocturnal rocker that is on the verge of blowing up. Such a narrative upends the bourgeois impediments of female drudgery: gone are the dollhouses, sewing machines, pudding and lollipops, and elusive flavors of girlhood. This is tough-ribbed, engineered rock'n'roll with whooshing, deep-release energy. The slower "Rip Me Up" is about the ratty feeling of being a 24-hour party person whose psyche is battered ("I've got nothing to hold me together anymore"). Rent may not be paid, but the narrator dreams of meeting the President while being kicked out as the guitars screech in a torrent.

Trick Babys were more propulsive, given the gargantuan grit and lungs of singer Lynne Von Pang (of Da Willys fame), who seemed to embody the larger-than-life grit of New York City itself. Her unparalleled voice should be required listening. It's like a mill-house churning out a refusal of gender norms.

The band was a fixture on the East Side, where they mingled in resale shops and record stores. Their music—tameless, quickening, and earmarked by humor—could veer from Didjits lightheartedness and hang-tight rhythms (often powerful as an H-Bomb), to Ramones-like urban surf familiarity. As such, "Phoney Macaroni" takes stabs at foreign cars. In fact, they launched their own version of "It's a Long Way Back," one of Dee Dee Ramone's artifacts from 1978, but are even more spirited on their hyper-potent version of "Your Phone's Off the Hook" by X, a cover tune that arguably overshadows the original.

Shonen Knife

As queens of fuzz-pop for over 35 years, Shonen Knife has been an uber-punk testament to international underground longevity, fan worship, and brilliantly unfussy tunes. Though their Japanese origins and sisterly bonds (the band features Naoko and Atsuko Yamano) deepen their unbuttoned and bubbling originality, their punk DNA is as molded from the Ramones (whose tunes like "Blitzkrieg Bop" and "Sheena Is a Punk Rocker" they cover with fresh-scrubbed relish, lullaby sweetness, and squirmy ease) as it is imprinted by Osaka city nights, perhaps pronounced most excitedly on titanic tunes like "Ramen Night" and kinetic "Osaka Rock City."

Few bands can remain so entranced and enthralled by punk's garage-rock promise. While thousands of bands have pretended to mimic the idea of punk "nuggets," Shonen Knife unroll infectious tunes, as identifiable, cool, and clever as ancestors ranging from ? and the Mysterians to the Buzzcocks. Their low-fi bubblegum "Lazybone" ("you don't need to be serious . . . you don't need to be nervous . . . I don't want to work a boring job") remains a convincing, slightly reclined outcry for a kind of joy that may disrupt aimless, heart-turned-to-cardboard workaday habits.

And, Shonen Knife is quite capable of unleashing their own metal-tinged heaviness, such as the driving force behind "Robots From Hell," which spotlights their transformability. It is followed by the totally crunchy, rumbling, hypnotizing exorcisms called "Monster Jellyfish" and "Jet Shot." Sonically, they recall the heyday of bands like Captain America / Eugenius, when vibrating, guitar-drenched pop overtures were the norm. That style contrasts with Shonen Knife's programmed, percolating, calculator techno "Capybara" as well as their wistful, lightly-shaded, nostalgia-buried "An Old Stationary Shop" and "Sunshine."

Their light-coated satire runs far and wide, including societal and gender flash points such as diets. In the bouncy and slightly messy musicality of "Diet Run," slender-seekers try to eliminate "superfluous flesh" in order to shape an ideal body, but such diets leave the narrator desperately desiring "sweets." Cravings for chocolate abound; however, the wiry tune's most hair-raising moment is the Lora Logic-esque saxophone (conjoined with guitar) solo that pours through the second half like mutant syrup, galvanizing the curious tune.

And just in case people automatically want to shrug off Shonen Knife as simpletons producing child-like ditties for portable record player beach crowds—think again. They are masters of mishmash cultural syncretism. I can hear critics whine, "Where are the menacing freakbeats like Ruin and Melt Banana, dude? Where are the gonzo, roving, harrowing geo-politico fireburners?" Shonen Knife do bring politics to the surface: in the rager "Economic Crisis," bleakness, revenge-modes, and animus are plenty evident as they deplore the hell caused by financial systems gone awry.

If ever a band was shaped by flux, by a passion for switching and trading genres (that need not be policed by too-cool goons), it is Shonen Knife. Their work ethic and perennial brain power have let them craft a tantalizing, startling catalog that oozes with earnestness, benevolent observational-wisdom, and wide-eyed pop culture commentary that does not shy away from social fault lines. Their music forms a kind of slot machine; it reveals wildly different combinations of moods, subject matter, and melody-making, but the band never gets caught in the quicksand of being forced, hackneyed, or phony.

The Wrecks, Dicks, Sister Double Happiness, Imperial Teen with Lynn Perko, Truell

P unk is littered with miles and miles of wreckage—suicides, failures, dropouts—but Lynn Truell (Perko) has been a remarkably persistent, talent-suffused, second-to-none drummer. She has thrived in a swelling reservoir of underground genres: the murky earlybird hardcore years of the Wrecks in hard-bitten Reno; the unrelenting, fortified agit-punk of the Dicks' second incarnation with gay front-man politico extraordinaire Gary Floyd; the blistering roots-rock and infectious intelligence of soul-harboring Sister Double Happiness, with Floyd at the helm; and the low-key, witty, indie rock of magnetic Imperial Teen.

Listening to the combustible, cataclysmic energy of "Teenage Jive" by the Wrecks is like eavesdropping on a drummer learning her trade in ferocious strides. The tunes are stop-start tantrums of abandoned norms. Gone are the twisted reggae grooves of the Slits, the quirk pastimes of the Raincoats, or the arty séances of Mydolls. This

equals brash, barren howls of combat-booted women tired of their kewpie doll upbringing and the lipstick routines of Farrah Fawcett look-alike America. "Don't even fuck with me cause I haven't got the time," they snarl. The recording is dingy, duct-taped, and noise-reeking, as if a seismograph of barely contained chaos. But the ethos is a fiery salute to all women breaking away from their towns, families, lovers, and soon to be burned and faded music collections. " I can't take it / where do I go to? . . . what am I gonna do?" they ask. As a band mostly gigging in the Sacramento/San Francisco area and landing a key track ("Punk is an Attitude") on the seminal *Not So Quiet on the Western Front* compilation, which featured the Dead Kennedys and MDC, they may be obscure, but their hungry sentiments and motifs cut deep.

When Truell appeared in the newly re-formed Dicks (a blasphemous version, according to some Texans, since the band was born in Austin with a different line-up), she brought an incredible fluid style. Tunes like "Sidewalk Begging" somehow combined dusty highway blues-barker vibes and a dire, cutthroat,

down'n'out San Francisco psyche into one spectacular howl of a tune, all pinned to the rhythm shaped by Truell's roving drum blasts. This one cut became a synecdoche for the band's sharp profile of abilities. The old Dicks sometimes felt like a battered jalopy of curt, even venal tunes, shaky shotgun rhythms, and politics as a fight with a broken bottle. In contrast, the new Dicks careened, still in the harsh sunlight, but re-tooled with Floyd's more confident and inexhaustible bluesy howls, bent-metal guitars, and drums flashing in rapid, flexing, sinewy succession.

Sister Double Happiness, on the other hand, seemed rooted in Floyd's small-town, railroad earth upbringing in places like Arkansas and Texas. It forged ties between accessible Creedence Clearwater Revival style roots-rock and the fixating psychedelic garage-rock of the 1960s. Still, Truell and company did not cease and desist their

political inclination. Their miraculous, churning "Freight Train" is largely acknowledged as the first rock'n'roll song to address the AIDs crisis: "I've got the plague of the century / it's like a freight train / like an airplane / like a hurricane." Plus, they gigged for Rock for Choice with Nirvana and L7 and paid homage to their radical past by covering "Holiday in Cambodia" by

Gary Floyd and Lynn Perko, provided by Gary Floyd

the Dead Kennedys. Never feeble, never tattered, never mere replicas of their former selves, and always fueled by grassroots tenacity, Truell and Gary Floyd raged against the dying of the light.

Imperial Teen saw Truell re-uniting with Jone Stebbins (The Wrecks) and changing her style from sheer loose-limbed powerhouse to more pensive and patient beats. This created a softer undergird for the band's adult pop aural cocktails. Truell's steadfastness is the perfect compliment to the band's catchy allure and queer sensibilities, especially on tunes like "Runaway." The band's penchant for carving novel, unisex-friendly, harmony-laden tunes like "Ivanka" put them in the rank and file of post-punks like B-52's, with all the cheekiness and wiry musical aptitude intact.

Bad Cop/Bad Cop

With toe-to-toe brawling brouhaha and pop-punk licks that spread like a quick disease, Bad Cop/Bad Cop are not a tonic but a testing ground. They effortlessly prove that the Fat Wreck Chords "sound" is as easily inhabited by young women ready to fight for justice, from street corners and bedrooms to the halls of power, as much as any tattooed boy. As such, they are a brand of accessible firepower.

"Sugarcane" announces their intentions with anvil-thick certainty, telling a victimized friend that if her malevolent boyfriend returns, the narrator will "use a fucking hammer on his face / yes I would do that for her." This demarcates girl power not as some abstract committee facing voter right issues or micro-aggression, but girl power dwelling and dueling in the same ratty clubs and tumbledown apartments as males steeped in machismo. This is a generation raised on The Distillers as much as feminist discourse, a generation ready to tackle the human garbage that still attempts to block females from their natural rights. "Get Up, Get Out, Get On" they urge, each member tackling the chorus in blitz-heroics, as if their very voices can carry the fight deep beyond ivy league campuses.

On the other hand, "Cheers" comes closer to mid-period Social Distortion and the Generators. It drips with a slightly punky-tonk vibe and more laid-back tempo behind a tale of inebriation and wounded relationships discovered in derelict dawns. As keen as California writers like John Fante, they sketch out the "smell of bleach and cheap shots / neon signs fluorescent flickers." The narrator readily admits to the deepest feelings—being emotionally stung, the awful taste on the tongue when recounting a name, the ugliness of being left behind. Yet, the song itself, like any great misery-soaked, country music gem, evokes a tale to be shared openly with all others that toil with similar loathing.

Having coped with a destructive relationship to booze, pills, and cocaine, singer/guitarist Stacey Kelvin Dee (of Angry Amputees and others too) has been sober for the last few years, as she explained to Smart Punk Live in 2016, which gives the tunes an extra biographic caliber. They come from a deeper marrow, carved from the often bitter circles of experience that can both dim the muses and prevent people from moving forward. Combining the efforts of family, band, and label, "It's been one heck of a year of self-discovery," she avowed, which led to reclaimed happiness. That determination seems to fuel some of the newer narratives, so instead of pictures of emptiness dotted with chaos and self-hate, the tunes feel like someone wrenched from the void, someone who has finally spotted modes of survival and unburied the truth.

That behind-the-scenes reality makes the band much more than scribes of popular punk, but a testament of being an effective tribe prepared to navigate the world's trip-wires and boobytraps. In all, they take a magnifying glass to the issues that pummel self-regard. They also depict all the exit wounds and in the end insert a kind of harnessed desire for change. All this upsets the status quo of being the bummed-out underdog, lacking power and resilience. Instead, through the sonic weaponry of punk, they restore and rectify what has been lost, challenged, and marred.

Nausea with Amy Miret

Just as New York City hardcore began its worldwide domination, another side of New York—the underground crust and Squat or Rot communities—was thriving, often with more women involved. Such was the case with Nausea, who gigged in front of banners declaring "No Housing No Peace." Their body of work melds the limber though heavy-hitting drumming of Amebix and Motorhead with tormented, gargled lyrics, with one exception: Nausea featured the frenzied ravings of Amy Miret, who helped inaugurate the era of bands featuring male-and-female grindcore, crossover, d-beat, and screamo singers.

For years, women had used their voices (starting most notably with Poly Styrene of X Ray Spex) to splinter notions of manufactured "femininity" (passivity, sweetness, obeisance, luxuriance) and turned music into a field of fire. In the case of Miret, on tunes like the surging, lawless "Godless," she attacks church and saviors, both the "holy water in a silver bowl" and "the sacred cross" that have delivered no more than "this living hell." To church-goers, she is a remorseless, sacrilegious iconoclast, berating the "Lord, god, father and son"; to agnostics and atheists, she is a freedom fighter, a serf metaphorically burning down an exploitative church.

With equally menacing, agile drums, and more adrenaline to attack higher beings, Nausea's most popular cut, "Cybergod," launches an attack on the digital/TV/media age, in which a "the warm static embrace" begins

to choke off a person's freedom. Why? Because falling under the spell, gaze, and commandments of the church (disguising itself as a provider of guidance and compassion) leads to being "baptized, chastised, desensitized, and lobotomized." The lyric's disdain festers like an open wound; the anger simmers like a cauldron. The merging of materialism, sin, and un-holiness—"naughty little girls . . . money and fast cars"—disgusts the narrator as the song reveals pastors using the tools of religion and pompous lies to fatten their own finances.

Other tunes are like dire, compressed poems re-tooled for complex hardcore, like "Here Today," which traces the devastation of natural areas from once fertile and verdant forest paths to clear-cut dead zones forming a "murdered biosphere." The eco-warning comes amid a nostalgia for the natural world before endless rampant harvesting, "manscapes" weighted with industrial waste, and polluted skies became a norm. Bands like Discharge were content to proffer stripped-down protests, no more than a few words duct-taped together and repeated ad nauseam, but Miret and crew explore sizzling poetics like "the raping of an eon's growth squandered callously." Such lines seem eerily Shakespearean in sentiment and style, not exactly what one might expect from grizzled-throats of crust punks.

And just as the Dead Kennedys took on corporatized youth music on "MTV Get Off the Air," Nausea locked onto the same target as well in "MTV (Feeding the Fortune 500)," itself a cunning wordplay on the Crass album *The Feeding of the 5000*. The narrative abhors the entertainment channel's "spew[ed] little psychodramas" and "endless token tantrums" keeping audiences "passive and desensitized." Much like televangelism is seen as the culprit in punk-centric movies like the 1980s cult classic *Repo Man*, which depicted an entire generation of middle-aged people inert and enervated, MTV was imagined as the great pacifier of youth in the 1980s. This was when Reagan committed war crimes, refused to deal with the AIDS crisis, and added fuel to the international East/West strife while also disemboweling the labor movement at home, all with a smile glued to his soon-to-be-senile face. Though MTV offered bits and pieces of dissent on shows like *120 Minutes* (videos by Gang Green, Bad Brains, Cro-Mags, Bl'ast), most of the channel's material spewed was fluff and "packed products" sold in endless "pantomimes," as Nausea lyrics remind us.

Bands like Nausea, dripping with bellicosity and frustration ("my rebellion's not for sale . . . so fucking go to hell!"), attempted to retain punk's outsider urgency and DIY ethos, all clothed in dark strife and potency. And Miret helped lead the women exposing the slimy, soiled eggwhite of big business, the burdens and feeble morality of repugnant religions, and the palpably wounded environment.

Go Betty Go

Sprung from the same electric furor that gave us the Runaways and the Donnas, Go Betty Go knows how to carve chrome-cool rock'n'roll as well as modern punk, though they were almost stalled mid-flight when singers switched out. Their well-annointed tunes flick powerfully through genres, including folk-meets-sea shanty tailspins on "The Pirate Song," ska-infusion on the glowing, powerful "Saturday" and even some nu metal undertones on the rock'en'español gone hardcore "*Son Mis Locuras.*" All of it proves the sisters Nicolette and Aixa Vilar and their companions are vivid wielders of deft musical chops.

Their album *Nothing Is More* features tons of roving, melodic, succinct tunes that act as warnings, like "Runaway": "You've got your priorities / Respect and loyalty / You've got your job and all your things / Your house and company." It encourages people to unhitch from their past to seek the things they truly love. They are also quite capable of cogent hardcore musical yearnings like "Get Out" that tell tales of street boys with guns navigating a maelstrom of sour relationships. With throbbing, top-notch rhythmic pace and howling vocals ("get out / get out"), the tune is drenched in urgency.

Still, their most impressive export is the unmatched confidence and drive of the loud-hailing EP *Worst Enemy*, beginning with the title song's summoning of high-voltage surf and plundering drums. While much rock can seem stilted and over-produced, this song actually delivers the blows with a blurred, vein-popping instinct and terrific furor. And the band defies the notion of punk being overly curt and truncated poetry by runaways and rejects. The lengthy "It's Too Bad," with its drilling rhymes ("Explanations / Hesitations / Suffocations / Frustrations / Limitations"), pictures the life of constricted women eager to shred shackles that bind, pinch, and attempt to mollify them. Like a flow of light igniting a new path, the song defies both suffocating personal attachments and the larger tentacles of a patriarchal world: "You can't have me!" they blare.

In 2015, they cut the *Reboot* EP with Emily Wynne-Hughes (who was an *American Idol* hopeful) as their new vocalist, emphasizing more rock-pop modes, like the Joan-Jett-echoing "It Haunts You Now." Still, some of their old punk'en'español fervor runs deep on driving tunes like "*Tartamudo*."

Meat Joy and F-Systems

Austin, TX was a fertile ground for an array of forward-thinking, clever, and high-caliber punks. But two seminal acts, F-Systems and Meat Joy, seem especially illuminating years later, like leitmotifs of the unruly era. And they deserve to be ushered into the annals of music history.

"People," the lean single by F-System, whose Lorenda Ash is behind the mic, is a synth-punk, new-wave-leaning gem that traces internalized media violence back to 1963, when John F. Kennedy was assassinated in downtown Dallas. "I can't feel anything / I don't touch anything / . . . I'm a walking wounded romance." Released in 1980, it feels like the dead-end of the Carter administration, when the nation seemed to be gripped by doldrums, insecurity, and stasis. The music is intensely gray and schematic, lacquered and orderly in its mechano-kinetic pulse, constricted, yet the vocals are blossoms of hurtled drama.

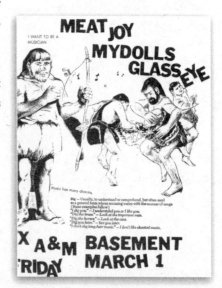

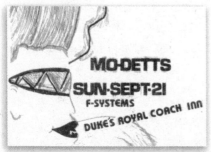

Then "Exorcism" is a novel eerie, jazzy-drummed, ghostly-guitar riddled slice of neo-Siouxsie and the Banshees fare: the murky atmospheric aesthetics get zippered with piecing, intersecting bass lines as Ash evokes "locked doors . . . violence . . . blood and pain . . . cages." It vibrates with a sense of ritualized, cathartic power and is a tune steeped in metaphoric residues of pain brought to bear on any slice of history when incarceration, sadism, and brutality were norms.

Meat Joy burst through the brick wall of punk conventions, finding a style that links to West Coast bands like the quirky Mutants and Pink Section as well as the specially queered theatrics of the B-52s during the late 1970s. But even more appealing is their interwoven, incredible jolting bass lines and zooming distorto-thickened guitar on tunes like "Slenderella," a piece of perverse musical logic that creates a surprising, terminal heaviness even as singer Gretchen Phillips mocks female stereotypes (a not-so-pretty picture of anorexics—woefully stylized death) with gleeful, hurtling caricatures. Plus, the band tucks Texas drawls into the mix as well.

The New Bloods with Osa Atoe

One of those carrying the progressive punk creed forward in the Deep South is Osa Atoe— journalist, singer, zine editor and writer of *Shotgun Seamstress*, community activist, organizer, and ceramicist who helped form the queer-allied, multicultural, all-female New Bloods in Portland. Soon, though, she moved to New Orleans. "I grew up in the suburbs of D.C., so the D.C. punk scene was the first one I experienced, starting in the late 1990s," she affirms. "So yes, Positive Force was influential to me (I even tried to join at one point!). Because I grew up around the D.C. punk scene and that was the first one I was exposed to, I always assumed that punk was a political thing. I didn't understand that punk could be nihilistic for awhile."

Though lacking the trademark guitar licks of trad punk, the New Bloods album *The Secret Life* (featuring counterparts Adee Roberson and Cassia Gammill) on Kill Rock Stars connects the dots between Lora Logic, Erase Errata, and other avant-garde thrill makers. The droning fiddle, displaced from a faraway front porch or a Velvet Underground outtake, together with unrestrained syncopated drums, make for an altogether otherworldly experience. This is punk deconstructed . . . elusive and elastic. "Oh Deadly Nightshade" veers from willowy, poetic ruminations about the death-delivering belladonna plant to sheer incantatory noise whirls and chants. It feels almost like rustic, bayou-drenched Sleater Kinney. Never pretentious or riddled with

Osa Atoe, New Orleans, 2014, by David Ensminger

fakery, it drifts in the mind, much closer to homegrown psych-punk than most paisley adorned bands of the 1980s.

"My entrance to punk rock was Riot Grrrl. I'd heard The Sex Pistols, The Clash, and NOFX before that, but it didn't make me feel like being a part of punk. Riot Grrrl did. So, I've always connected punk rock to issues of social justice. Positive Force and Fugazi were just more ways in which punk and politics were shown to me to be inseparable. My political awakening and my love for punk rock kind of grew concurrently. I wasn't ever introduced to apolitical punk. I very naively did not realize that there were people out there that thought that punk was just about getting wasted and offending people."

"In 2007, my band New Bloods played a benefit show I set up for the New Jersey 4, a group of black lesbians who were sentenced to prison for defending themselves against a homophobic and racist attack. I do ongoing benefits for Community Kitchen, a Food-Not-Bombs-like group that serves free meals underneath City Hall every week here in New Orleans. Plus, I run No More Fiction as a way to get more women and LGBTQ+ folks to participate in DIY and punk music making. If the show I set up isn't to support a touring band, it is a benefit for a local cause. Another gig benefited Pink & Black, a LGBTQ+ prisoner support and prison abolition group in New Orleans."

Her newest venture in the city, Negation, which featured Osa on bass and vox, is brutal dirge-drummed artcore that lands somewhere in-between Unwound and Red C (with fellow female punk Toni Young). Heady tunes like "The Soul is the Prison of the Body" tumble into the ear with lo-fi collateral damage, while "Son Of No One" wraps the talk-sing declaratives "he's so fucking twisted / he hates almost everyone" around bass drum jackhammer pounding and feedback-drenched, circulatory guitar. It erupts venal, noise-splintered, searing, and deadly, as if the very embodiment of total cynicism.

For the likes of Atoe and myriad others, punk conscience and outreach are not a history lesson scrawled in stone somewhere out of reach. They amount to living lessons, a life-blood, which provides a reason to make music, a reason to gather, and a reason to steer the community towards better alternatives than the clanging jostle of beer bottles at the local dive bar, with its enforced age barriers, profit aimed bottom-line, cavalier apolitical vibes, and business-as-usual practices. Atoe believes in punk's transformational credentials and potential, not just "resting-on-my-laurels" subcultural lore. She is the frontline of hope in the genre.

Marian Anderson of the Insaints and Eva von Slut of Thee Merry Widows

In punk, the body itself is invariably cast as a site of political discourse, freedom anchored in flesh brought to bear in cases like the arrest of Marian Anderson, who was also known as Seaweed and Swamp Thing. She was the subject of the documentary *Punk Goddess* and a Dionysian-style singer of the band Insaints and later the Thrill Killers. She was also arrested for lewd behavior at Gilman Street (the club that gave rise to Green Day) in Berkeley in 1993 for offending the "heterosexual rights" of religious-minded Carlos Cadona, known as 6025, a former member of the Dead Kennedys.

Anderson was a counterculture icon in her community: she appeared in *Sadobabies: Runaways in San Francisco* (named after the dolls that serve as abused avatars for the traumatized teens) in 1988 and on the cover of *the Spectator* ("California's Weekly Sex News and Review"); gigged alongside the likes of the Offspring and Rancid; released a vinyl 45 with the Insaints (infernal tunes like "Loser's Club," "Stupid Boy," and "Whore"); and overcame family sexual abuse, self-cutting, bipolar disorder, suicide attempts, group homes, juvenile hall, squats like the Polytech High School, and more to revel on stage in the manner of anything-goes GG Allin. During gigs, Anderson, who dated Tim Yohannon of *Maximum Rocknroll* for a short time, regularly pushed the borders of "good taste," even within punk territories. "We'd invite other girls that she worked with [as a dominatrix] to do sexual acts onstage with her. Fist fucking and pissing, we had shows where dildos were involved. Bananas were going all weird different places," recalls guitarist Daniel DeLeon (Boulware and Tudor 2009).

Due to the Gilman's "private club" status—people attending shows needed to have a membership card—Anderson beat the charges against her, which the district attorney dropped. She was helped by Ann Brick of the American Civil

Flyer from Collective Chaos

Liberties Union and civil rights attorney George Walker. Sadly, Anderson died from a heroin overdose in 2001.

"I grew up in a small Midwestern town. I grew up surrounded by religion, and what I felt was a stifling atmosphere where I felt enormous pressure to 'fit in,'" tells Miss Eva von Slut of Thee Merry Widows / White Barons, who was invited by Daniel DeLeon, Insaints guitarist and now a psychobilly fellow traveler, to front the tribute version of the Insaints. "I just was not able to do so; I was a weird kid who liked strange stuff like horror movies. Later on, I got into punk rock and threw myself wholeheartedly into underground music. I was a regular reader of *Maximum Rocknroll* in my teen years, and I ached to be in a place like the Bay Area, where freedom of expression was not only allowed but encouraged. So, reading about women like Marian Anderson and Wendy O. Williams was nothing short of a miracle. I remember reading about Marian and being struck by the fact that she was creating music and art on her own terms and was willing to accept the consequences for where her art took her.

"In the pre-YouTube days, I was never able to see any footage of the Insaints, but I did order their split 7-inch record with the Diesel Queens and was blown away by both the music and the words. When Marian sang 'I Am a Whore' in her fabulously spiteful voice, I got shivers down my spine . . . . Although the onstage sex shenanigans are what people talked most about, the music stands up on its own as great punk rock. Her voice was powerful but feminine. I think she is a very underrated punk rock frontwoman," affirms von Slut.

Above all, Miss Eva still finds power and perseverance in Marian's candid clamor. "Obviously, Marian was enjoying finding ways to assert her sexuality onstage. She was a woman showing she was beautiful and sexual and could not be pushed around. That was one of the biggest things that attracted me to the Insaints—the obvious enjoyment of being 'in your face' about sex and the control that shines through in Marian's vocals and lyrics. I don't ever recreate what Marian did onstage, as that isn't my thing, and I feel as though that would be almost disrespectful of what Marian was doing as an artist. We do usually incorporate some kind of nod to her onstage performances. For instance, I had some friends from the Lusty Lady perform some striptease onstage with us a few shows back. The most recent Insaints show had a burlesque performance with a banana incorporated into the show. I think you can't separate Marian's sexuality from her music, and although her story ends tragically, her strength and resilience in the face of a terrible upbringing are something many women can identify with. She remains one of the true icons of underground punk rock in my mind."

Vice Squad with Beki Bondage (Rebecca Louise Bond)

In the early 1980s, punk oscillated between genres and categories that often held little regard for each other. Second wave bands began to peak while the 'year zero' bands sometimes lost the confidence of wayward youth. Into the void stepped Vice Squad, led by Beki Bondage, who has towered over street-punk-meets-metal ever since. To some of the older crowd, these punks seemed no more than groveling, grinding, glue-sniffing guttersnipes who attracted Mohicans and skinheads infatuated with power'n'violence. Such music symbolized a triad of problems: lowly performances, handicapped style, and backsliding aesthetics, critics might argue. Missing from the second wave was the Rosetta stone of punk: breakthroughs, discoveries, and strange fixations. In its place was militant working class aggression cloaked in studded leather jackets, thick-toed glistening boots, spiked hair, pathological machismo, and swift wrongheadedness that kept many women sidelined from the chutes of power. Yet Bondage helped rectify and remedy that situation: in her lyrical hands, street punk was an anti-depressant to the times. She exuded a black market of youth dreams, a place to cope with tribal anxieties, and a social language that dealt with the threats, exhaustion, ironies, and stress. She also deftly described the Cold War conflict unraveling in the Thatcher/Reagan years.

By 1980, Vice Squad released stupendous fare like the hectic, mid-paced "Living on Dreams," which took stabs at the revolution rockers embedded in punk crowds: "Revolution in your living room / Revolution in your home / You can stick your revolution / I'm much better on my own." She does not belt out Trotskyite ranting or a communist manifesto: she testifies to individual volition and choice. When sectarian politics began ingratiating itself into the punk community, some welcomed the furor, but others saw the intrusion as lame. And long before bands like Sluts for Hire and Pansy Division glommed the world of sexual underground/fetish/carnality onto punk's blotched surfaces, Bondage was singing "Latex Love," name dropping all the kinks that would spook pastors—"rubber scrubbers . . . breathing tubes . . . bullwhip . . . gas masks." This is the stuff of fetishistic German porno films, rarely heard in punk's bullhorn.

Their magnum opus is "Last Rockers," a vivid apocalyptic vision of a world tattered by war caused by politicians doing things "no god can forgive." "All we ever wanted was to be free / Our music was our only joy / And the government wants to search and destroy," Bondage contends as the song finally musters a despondent ending—a few guitar lines warble into nothingness. It fits well into punk's catalog of despair and visions of government-as-malevolent force, but more importantly, the song structure proved their generation could convene a high-yielding creative force.

One of their other memorable achievements is their unwavering positive commitment to youthful bonds, resourcefulness, and togetherness exalted on "Stand Strong Stand Proud." On it, Bondage reproaches the parent/teacher/boss substrata that molds conformity, especially when adolescence is left behind: "They'll tell you now you're old enough / You should settle down / They'll take away your dignity." As a gem from 1983, it features waterfalls of tom-toms, turbid guitars, and cranked-up bass.

For decades now, the band has merged metal's thick walls of heavily chorded assault with intransigent punk attitude and velocity. They've even faithfully covered "Enter Sandman" by Metallica and "Ace of Spades" by Motorhead. Plus, in the scope of her lyrics, Bondage continues to navigate the complex travails of personal relationships, like "Spitfire." It bemoans pigheaded partners: "You time with me was your finest hour / I ain't your meal ticket anymore / and the shit you write is your only power / you're just a wanna-be media whore." In one lyric, she deftly alludes to World War II airpower, betrayals of trust, and the contemporary digital landscape of the media-industrial complex. Each pictures a sense of bombardment and victimhood.

"Blokes always dominated women," Bondage told a television camera in 1983. "I am going to dominate men instead." She demonstrated this on albums like *Defiant* in 2006, featuring fine lyrics like "free speech is against the law / now we're all criminals." Her antagonism towards central authorities and bloated bureaucracies remains the aim of her lyrical sniper scope. She castigates "the vultures," in Bondage's parlance, that "cover up and sanitize the cruel and obscene" and scrutinizes the dirty dealings happening in conference rooms that led to the Iraq War.

Such invectives remain unabated, and her sympathies still gravitate towards those in the street, clamoring for hope and freedom. The music may sound more thoroughly produced and crossover metal-punk with a populist, anger-mismanagement streak. Still, it keeps all the ethos of the 1980s stoked and tended, shaped by Bondage's formidable intelligence, sweeping concerns, and musical development.

Capitol Punishment with Joceylin Fedrau

Like other brazen women in the 1980s, Joceylin Fedrau helped destabilize calcified gender roles by proving hardcore was not just boys' fun. Though the band itself has been much underappreciated over the decades, their work reverberates in stark contrast to simple, stripped down fare.

Their 1986 opus *Slum with a View* offers a jumbo slice of their skills. Lyrics, mostly written by gravel-mouth singer Ralph Lotspeich, roam the wasteland of America, eyeing all that is problematic and woeful. This includes the ghettos on the title track in which people are "stuck to paper like a fly" as they cope with "cracks in floors, doors and walls / smashed pipes and darkened halls." The whole depiction feels downright Dickensian.

"Huelga," though penned thirty years ago, broods over dire 21st century issues: the band pays witness to the bedraggled, underdog workers "bent over in field / back about to break / putting food on everybody

else's plate." Though they s t r u g g l e in the breadbasket of the country, the thick midsection of California, immigrants are food insecure. They are barely able to feed their own families while picking cheap produce for supermarkets aplenty. This tune is no fake reporter's job; these are people the band saw everyday in the "105 degrees . . . dust . . . [and] chemicals" near their home turf of Fresno, CA. Note Fedrau's tightly unfolding, walking bass lines and the drummer's sudden shift to jazz-like bongo syncopation in the break as well. Fedrau was a super-concentrated, inventive,

shrewd player who balanced the guitar crunch and cacophony of equally intense Dale Stewart. Though writers may continually skip their mention or miss their heyday, Capitol Punishment remains a severely talented crew who chose to keep punk's promise of being unorthodox even as the genre suffered from a cookie cutter mold. In doing so, they rise above the trash heaps and broom closets of history and seem as timely as ever, for they probed systems of control; bleak, marooned, exploited immigrants; out-of-control tyrants; pockmarked landscapes; and devastated, dead-end inner cities. Such narratives alone concretize their place in the halls of punk infamy.

The Germs with Lorna Doom (Teresa Ryan)

The Germs were the Dionysian wrecking ball that helped create the reality-TV aspect of punk debauchery: the lurid smashed glass, inebriation, self-mutilation, and occultishness the media craved so much. Yet, behind the melee was a formidable musical experience, distilled into (im)perfection on (GI), their strongest fare. With Lorna Doom pulling the bass levers, the album's deadly oeuvre tugs on the battered boot heels of greatness. The purging opener "What We Do Is Secret" unlocked a hardcore blueprint: compared to first wave punk that sometimes plodded along in an upbeat, unsteady haze, the Germs' debut full-length had a relentless, menacing rhythm mixed with magnetic poetry. That drew from the dizzying talking points of a smartly enraged, meaty tongued, often slurred and elbow-pushing Darby Crash. The pulsebeat is intense, pressing, unashamed, conspicuously surging, which is most pronounced on other tunes like "The Slave." The brainy lyrics mirror a cultivated sense of outsiderness: "standing in the line we're aberrations / defects in a defect's mirror / and we've been here all the time real fixations / hidden deep in the furor."

If you wonder how punk devolved into the noisy late-SST period look no further than "Shut Down [Annihilation Time]," launched with Doom's trudging, lurching bass. The song is as alarming as the early Stooges, when all pop-a-delic pretense went AWOL. This is brooding, hammer swinging, brutal-forged slow motion. The ratty vocals of Crash, which begin with a sense of 19th century poetic conceits ("let me touch the tips of inculcated desire / and brush the fettered veil away") soon devolve into sizzling, hissyfit, sputtering rants dispensing rampant, uncontrollable desire: "now I want / your soul, lemme get control."

In turn, Doom threads through the ruckus on "Media Blitz" with ceaseless vibrancy as Crash enumerates all that remains suspect, ill, and threatening about the media-industrial sphere ("don't steal your eyes off the TV screen / Can you realize we're what we've seen / take an injection from the mad machine"). The band charges, "We are what we ate from the televised blitz." In the age when "the media is the message / mess age" was firmly engaged by the counterculture, the Germs understood the inherent curse of it all: "We're vision rapers and we seed the signs / You'll play your part in the master mind."

Rezillos /Revillos' Fay Fite (Sheila Hynde)

With upstart firepower, complete tunefulness, and unabashed smarts, the Rezillos were a huge force concurrent with punk's first tidal wave of inventive fare. Melded at the hip with partner Eugene Reynolds, Fay Fife infused punk with crazed grit and memorable commotion, proving their TV and vinyl record-obsessed childhood made fertile ground for reinterpretation and rejuvenation when they became adults.

The band remorselessly examines hi-fi stereos, stock markets, TV programs spruced up with lip syncing stars, fashion ware, and slapdash money people accrue while seeking their fifteen minutes of fame. As Fife sings, "I'll do anything if that's the right thing to see . . . Sing song, then fade away." As they suggest, the bloated, self-serving music industry is a revolving door of desire and disappointment, leisure society faux-drama, and fake programming that lulls the masses. Consumers are led like sheep by hollow celebrities. The song's tenor and insight are truly riveting; ironically, they played the song on *Top of the Pops* (which itself contained canned/fake/prerecorded musical performances) in 1978.

With a B-movie sci-fi imagination wildly at play, "Flying Saucer Attack" and "Destination Venus" reach the outer limits of cinematic goofiness and foreshadow their aesthetic to come after the band's mutation into the Revillos in 1979. Both bands inhabit the realm of chrome spaceships, laser beams, radio frequencies, and infinite miles stretching between far off planets. It acts as a revolt of incredulity: when the world becomes bland, run by sedate officious functionaries and crammed with sky-rises doubling as air-conditioned jail cells, space becomes the place. For children born into the Cold War period of Soviet-American rocket races, the bands offered a gripping soundtrack packed with unfaltering energy, abrupt changes, mixed-sex vocal-trade offs, Reynolds' raspy élan, and Fife's exhilarating dash.

SECRET MUSIC PRESENTS

THURSDAY 18th DECEMBER
8:00pm

DELTA 5
ESSENTIAL
LOGIC
VINCENT UNITS

Acklam Hall Acklam Road W10
Tickets: £2 from Rough Trade or at door

Delta 5 with Ros Allen (originally from the Mekons), Julz Sale, and Bethan Peters!

Definitely part of the post-punk artcore brigade alongside the Slits, Raincoats, Gang of Four, Mydolls, and Bush Tetras, these Leeds-based insurrectionists mine the idiom ceaselessly. Foremost, and off-putting to some, they use curious vocals that seem easily at home in the plays of Samuel Beckett, as well as distant relatives of Dada theater. Language itself becomes a focus and fulcrum, a field of ideas exchanged and examined, a place of constant play, inversion, and deconstruction. As such, the band feels less like a punk barrage and more like trance at times—in "You" (armed with bird-like calls of "you, you, YOU"), with its locked-up drumming,

slanted shambolic guitar, and bass that weaves back and forth effortlessly as a fishing line. It's a wonderful pointed (but not dreadfully severe) analysis of disappointing and rigged gender roles ("who was seen with somebody else . . . who forgot to phone last Tuesday . . . who likes sex only on Sundays . . . you!"). Like a newspaper column, they relish the candid telegraphing of truths.

"Try" mimics a similar set of repeated lines, though the guitar is a bit more hardened and clipped, and (two!) bass lines pounce as the lyrics unfold ("try try . . . it's an effort to confide . . . I don't want to be a problem . . . you don't see what I see"). The narrative thrust seems to revolve around bifurcated points of view—each angled in such a way to cause blind spots and resentment. The lyrics don't try to bleed emotions. They try to frame the argument, to get to the heart of the issue, to the gray everyday dynamics of faulty relationships. This is not pathos-tinged, feeling-blue country music. This is a dialectical undertaking.

The BBC called their vocals "detached, conversational," but the syntax does not sound like inebriated dribble heard around a pub, nor do they seem to keep each other at arm's length. Instead, to me, they feel like they are hashing out prose back and forth, leaping in and out of each other's thoughts. This creates a feminist form that is decidedly different than typical rock prose and patter.

Plus, they were fervent left-wingers often in the service of Rock Against Racism; hence, they were not armchair avant-gardists waiting for the new nation to arise. They were heady protagonists on the streets, stirring the conversations. They fought intolerance and injustice one irreversible chord at a time, thereby creating discourse among the discord of the late 1970s-early 1980s.

Lydia Lunch

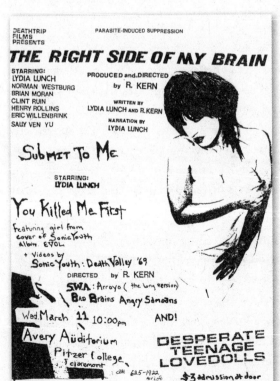

Discussing Lunch, I suppose, automatically invites her wrath and chagrin. But I will try, for she models all that is bewitching and bewildering, and she is a permanent fixture of transgression with more ties to Dada than punk rock. Well, at least that is true in terms of her curating a conceptual, ongoing, and chaotic assault on all things status quo.

She first began performing in public at an acid party in upstate New York, then channeled her love of cock rock and glam as a 14 year-old by haunting New York City's "bankrupt and dangerous" streets, including attending gigs by the New York Dolls. But when she stumbled upon Suicide, their scorched glass punk muzak changed her direction and focus. As a result, she helped launch No Wave. That is a loose-knit term that she defines as user non-friendly, non-melodic, confrontational, and fashion-less . . . it is more attuned to psychological states of the makers than road maps of music. As such, the genre / tag lets loose a musical babble of broken guitar, "fascistic beats," and instinctually combative tunes in Teenage Jesus and the Jerks, which helped imprint a new way of musical existence. Alongside co-perpetrators on the scene like Arto Lindsay, James Chance, and more, such mayhem makers felt indissolubly connected with people as much as non-existent manifestos.

Even in 2008, when the band re-emerged with Thurston Moore at places like the Knitting Factory, they were more than a redux slamming of forefingers agitating tortured guitar strings—they were a force of nature segmenting life from then/now. In the moment, enduring the tunes, one shivers: the moment is irreducible, amputated from everything, in-between time. Every other genre, even the rugged directness of punk, felt sluggish, futile, dammed up with mud, in comparison to the dark theater and tumult of the Jerks on the ear-bleeding "Burning Rubber." It represents a complete fracture from "lady" voice: gone are folk refrains, soft lullabies, woozy disco, and shiny happy pop. This is the deplorable female renegade in sonically disheveled schizo musical prowess. Meanwhile, on "This Side of Nowhere," (1981) a Goth mystique is overlaid on her dark visions, "Dead still the hour in the middle of the day / Dead still the horror in the middle of the day," she sings.

Along with punk writer Kathy Acker and others, and deeply inspired by literary anti-heroes like Henry Miller, Hubert Selby, and Marquis de Sade, she became one of the prime voices of lit-punk, spoken word, and post-new journalism. Acker remained unafraid to pull back the Teflon shield of everyday life and see the ugliness underway—to do so, she documented "her personal insanity, and the political insanity happening at the time," as she told a UMass Amherst Library audience. Or, as she told an Australian host in 1994, she is the one to address "personal history of abuse, familial dysfunction, sexual obsession, the American way of life . . . " in a series of protests that propel her whole life. As a small child, she witnessed riots in Rochester that in some way spurred her to speak up against the three oppressive fathers: biological, religious, and national.

Lydia Lunch was a shattering prose writer at her core, and her album *Queen of Siam* feels like it could exist in the middle of a set by the Lounge Lizards or wayward Tom Waits. The storylines stubbornly curve through urbane, low-key free jazz and mutant ambience, in sync with moods, but not necessarily owned by them. The spontaneity of the playing is offset by her insistent, heavy-breathing language that foreshadows the work of Nick Cave. On the other hand, "Atomic Bongos" is anti-disco dripping with driving drums, propulsive push, bass-threaded rumble, and scurvy, skittery guitar offering sheer moments of combustion.

The next years offered fare that maneuvered to change pop and rock forever, with only slightly less caustic approaches, like the brilliant, cursed, apocalyptical noise escapades of "Death Valley 69" (in which Lunch teams up with Sonic Youth). It teemed with mutilated song form and gruesome video depictions, all caught by director Richard Kern, the bad boy Andy Warhol of noise in New York, who featured her in disturbing, outlandish, grueling short films that rankle and disgust normals, liberals, feminists, and reactionaries alike. To true believers, he was considered an outsider genius of horror porn, midnight movie, and cinema punk verite who squished bad taste into avant-garde traditions that reached back to *Un Chien Andalou*, the 1929 film by Luis Bunuel. Harebrained academics might see Kern films as abject grotesqueries, just as they might envision Kembra Pfahler, another one of his subjects, as one too, due to her vagina being sewn shut in a 1992 performance piece. Hence, all these acts relate more to Antonin Artaud's sense of 'theater of cruelty' than to Riot Grrrl dictums.

She continues as Lydia Lunch Retrovirus, with malcontent composer Weasel Walter of The Flying Luttenbachers as her schizoid guitar sidekick. Unabated, fearless, intrepid, unnerving to many, she will always remain cataclysmic, a bender of rules.

The Soviettes with Annie 'Sparrows' Holoien, Susy Sharp, and Maren 'Sturgeon' Macosko

In the line of other great Minneapolis bands ranging from Suicide Commandos to the 1990s family of Selby Tigers and Dillinger Four, the Soviettes exuded a tough, brazen synergy that incorporated lean hydro-powered pop and punk's zealous, mercurial side.

"Multiply and Divide" remains their towering achievement, a cult-inducing stab of music. The lyrics, dizzy with intelligence and swipes at American pride, implore listeners to find ways to resist conformity and acquiescence ("Learn! How to think things through / and things you can do to fight") and kick monotonous domesticity to the curb ("Put the keys to the house / at the end of the circle then you'll see / that you stuck to the plan"). No pill or plan will suffice because unhappiness breeds underneath the clean, smooth surface of it all, they insinuate—the sheen of manufactured monoculture is paper-thin.

Their forceful rock'n'roll chops are plenty evident on multiple tunes, like the harmony-strewn "Paranoia Cha Cha Cha!" Lyrically, the us-versus-them street scene illustrates the uncomfortable truth about monitoring difference and otherness. The tune highlights creepy mentalities that arise when people's sense of tolerance and togetherness gives way to a poisonous framework of divisiveness and scapegoating. While the band delivers this through metaphor and blunt dialog ("He doesn't look like you? Call us, we'll get him!"), it is nonetheless a disquieting slice of flash fiction about what happens when civility erodes.

Other times, they shed light on the confusing times of youth navigating desire, relationships, and tarnished reputations ("sometimes in little games, we end up getting lost"). Such sentiments make up ordinary (but still unpleasant) heart bleeding, woeful regret, and stirred-up spite, which is visited in other tunes like "Hot Sauced and Pepper" as well. In more dramatic surges, tunes like "#1 is Number Two" visit the quagmire of success, in which reaching the peak still means feeling "let down" (because it's never enough). The band's unrelenting honesty is resolute.

Further tunes like "There's A Banana In My Ear" are prescient, genuine, and decidedly adept at segueing from issues like geo-politics and press manipulation to economic pressures and conformity. They sew together a number of clichés ("They hate us for our freedom . . . always trust the state . . . the papers wouldn't print what isn't true") to show how hegemony operates—not through a series of powerful measures and government decrees, but through inner-colonization. People become more self-satisfied, and the masses tune out instead of thinking critically. Hence, citizens wipe their hands of blood spilled at their expense, here and abroad. Like "see no evil, hear no evil, speak no evil" (in the tune, it becomes "No-one can be blamed for what no-one ever knew"), people are cocooned in a Teflon world while those stuck outside "hate us for what we've done."

In these tremendous, visceral moments, the band's explorations of modern life shake up the standards of the punk-pop format. The band is a full representation of punk's forces: they offer up uncomplicated, charged, bubblegum diversions with piled-up brio while tackling the socio-economic and cultural woes of the present day. Maren "Sturgeon" Macosko went on to join the Gateway District, whose torso-shaking rock'n'punk was captured in leather jacket grit on albums like *Some Days You Get the Thunder*, while Susy Sharp joined the sly, catchy, garage-rock slamming That's Incredible.

Fifth Hour Hero with Genevieve Tremblay

Cutting across the national borderline with their heady Canadian post-hardcore punk, Fifth Hour Hero, with Genevieve Tremblay at the vocal helm, were tuneful, roughly melodic, speedy without mimicking hyper-punk push, and passion-packed to the gills. Their early albums like *Scattered Sentences* and *Collected in Comfort* set the tone, pace, and style. Tunes range from quieter slices such as "The Line" to the slower-treading syncopation, chopped-up emo structure, and guitar menagerie of "With Such Rights." The result is often breathtaking—youthful, but sophisticated and absorbing.

Still, Not Revenge . . . Just a Vicious Crush is an even more rigorous undertaking that pushes hard and fast from the get-go, like the bluesy micro-ramble that soon shapeshifts into their fierce "Playing Politics," an indefatigable slice of punk. It unveils Hollywood's control apparatus, which tries to keep the dream machine of a "perfect world" going by keeping reality at bay, suppressing opinions ("not allowed") and cracking down, if needed ("the streets put on their riot dress"). As a thunderous groundswell that begins the album, it amounts to a torrent of truth-to-power, a plea to unhitch hegemony's picture show. "Faint and Fading Out" barely gives up any of the velocity and sweep, though this time the narrative turns introspective with slight instilled tinges of ennui and personal regret: "I've been flirting with disaster / acting as the mistress of happiness." And such guises can only last so long before dissatisfaction grows deep and profound. The end goal is "constancy" and "goddamn honesty," which means no longer drowning in charades—if so, one might figuratively turn "blue" as real hopes get squandered. By navigating such distress, the tune becomes a wake-up call to the listener: smell the coffee, seek the truth, and free yourself, lest you become just another witness.

The stupendous, roiling drumming on "Coeur de Berlin" pumps the rhythm hard and fluidly, just as the vocals offer a perspective on their southern neighbors, the U.S.A., which only feigns to believe in compassion and really has "the world crawling under [its] jurisdiction." That template for neo-colonial control, though, has obviously withered. "You swallow excuses in fame and confusion," they posit, seeing the hubris of a country that pretends its priorities and desires are best for the globe. Lyrics like "We'll cut the veins that run through our Berlin heart," are poignant, but abstract sentiments, perhaps suggesting that the invisible barrier with Canada is as real and sometimes marked by pain as the collapsed wall that divided Germany in the Cold War. All in all, Fifth Hour Hero exudes a kind of ardent vigor and weighty insight that never grows staid or po-faced. Tremblay went on to join the catchy, nuanced Rome Romeo (try "Black Tape"), in which her strong, soaring voice came close to an updated version of Chrissie Hynde (the Pretenders). Then she shaped the even more "mature" and mainstream-leaning Abbesse (try their gem "Lit Up"). The latter produces both confident, smooth, dramatic delivery à la the Kills and brims with tunefulness that exudes strong hints of 1980s acts like Romeo Void and the Cure.

The Voluptuous Horror of Karen Black with Kembra Pfahler

Pfahler, known for her shock troop The Voluptuous Horror of Karen Black, dared to blur the lines between transgressive performance art, disturbing cinema, haywire experimental theater, pop culture insurrection, and punk antagonism. Sister of Adam Pfahler, the drummer of Jawbreaker, she has carved out concepts such as Availabism (making use of material at hand, which she describes as an "anti-classist, socialist tool") and Anti-Naturalism. As a manifesto maker and scion channeling the likes of Butthole Surfers, GG Allin, Lydia Lunch, and Wendy O. Williams, she venerates the path less traveled.

Whether sewing her vagina shut in the Richard Kern film *The Sewing Circle* or cracking eggs on it, her body has become an unhindered art-zone indebted to a teenage life spent watching bands like the Screamers, Suicide, and Swans, but even more importantly, female punks. "The punk rockers in Los Angeles were very advanced in their gender politics. Women were treated very differently than we see today," she told *Punk Globe*. "There were androgynous women, saucy women, big girls, small girls, and the concept of beauty was not cliche at all. I feel like the women who were involved in those bands integrated with the boys." Pfahler used this fluid and flexible gender playland as an interzone in which she could explore the nuances, risks, damage, fault lines, and taboo areas of social acceptance, musical expression, and life-as-art.

Musically, in an era rife with Hedwig and the Angry Inch, the Toilet Boys, and other genre/gender benders, The Voluptuous...sounds like gonzo molten metal ("PLOW," "Dionetics," "Chopsley: Rabid Bikini Model"), campy tongue-in-cheek divergent rock'n'roll ("I Believe in Halloween," "Neighborachie," "One Man Lady"), and irreverent punk with a gruff Plasmatics onslaught ("Underwear Drawer") that hearkens back to the devious anything-goes bedlam of

Lunachicks and Tribe 8. The entire catalog feels restless, unpredictable, screwball and outrageous.

In her conceptual art (which blurs the fine line between film, life, and stage), the body is polluted and deconstructed—bloodied, mutant, and flux-ridden, imminently weird and foreign. She employs a warped, sci-fi kind of Kabuki stylization. The body becomes a site of endless procreativity, a continuous remaking of the self, which relates to how transsexuals (whom Pfahler has called "far more courageous than an academic art movement" to *Punk Globe)*, genderqueers, and others create identities that are fluid and full of flux.

Instead of exploring mere gender, though, Pfahler—sometimes adorned with a massive wig, painted red skin, and full leg boots—embodies sheer otherness. She transcends junk culture materialism, for her body acts as a conduit for enigma and explosity, a re-thinking of pop culture. Hence, she has earned a place at alternative art galleries, the Whitney Biennial, and the garden of Monet's Giverny Gardens (in collaboration with E.V. Day). Her iconic look in the art environment was inspired by *Playboy*'s illustration known as Femlin by LeRoy Neiman. She presented "an interesting alien injection into the almost Disneyland-esque, iconic landscape of Giverny," wrote The Hole's press release. For many, Pfahler is disquieting, unsettling, and freakishly deviant, but she fits into a spectrum of punk whose purpose is to undo all that is considered "natural," "feminine," and "appropriate." In doing so, she is the one that buckles the straight world, plays havoc with borders in music, self, art, and society, and lets us all become passengers on her path of disorder and re-imagination.

Spitboy

On the Lookout roster, typically a refuge for garage rock redux and pop-saturated punk, Spitboy was the closest act akin to Crass' *Penis Envy* period. As such, they were a defiant bunch, a posse of feminists led by singer Adrienne Droogas and Xicana drummer and memoirist Michelle "Todd" Cruz Gonzalez, who eschewed speed for pummeling polemics. Harnessing a desire to crush repressive norms, they are inspired by the likes of feminist philosopher Sandra Lee Bartky, the cutting edge of theory from decades back who articulated a dissent against everyday, all-encompassing gender control systems, including regimes of skinniness and shame, self-loathing, and self-criticism that beset women, especially across the Western world.

Even a single album felt monumental. Each became like a treatise of how to practice decontrol and begin to deconstruct and dismantle the male consciousness, with its codes of power that offer up a "paradisiacal" harmony of alpha man and subservient woman. Their songs become attacks on these constructed notions of such an imbalance of power disguised as the natural, God-given order.

Musically, they brim with methodical, abrasive, even menacing rhythms, and semi-repetitive onslaughts. Thus, they seem slightly less interested in revolutionizing the sonic sphere than inserting their footprint, and conscience, into the framework of contested punk spaces. The stomping, groaning minimalism allows for the vendetta-vocals and sizzling polemics to take center stage, which forever shaped the post-1990s punk continuum. As such, they are a tour-de-force, both of pure energy and steely nerves, brimming with hardcore vigor.

Patricia Morrison of the Bags, Gun Club, Sisters of Mercy, and the Damned

Patricia Morrison is one of the most elusive punk women. She is daunting to discuss, and not because she hasn't given decades of her life to punk culture, music, and fashion. Documenting her presence and vital contributions takes a winding path. In the end, though, she remains one of punk's founding forces in America, a hero of the blank generation.

As early as 1976, as "Pat Bag," she helped form the Bags with Alice Bag, creating that peculiar, proto-hardcore template on quintessential singles like "Survive" from 1978, which has earmarked the band in official "must-have" punk catalogs. By 1981, Morrison swept into Legal Weapon, who would later become a mainstay of metal-esque Hollywood Boulevard sleaze rock'n'roll with a punk twist. But on their brilliant *No Sorrow* EP, anchored by 'Patricia Rainone's' thudding, deft bass lines, especially on

the turbulent "Pow Wow," they produce an inchoate blend of punk and off-kilter, formidable rock'n'roll, and the vocals of Kat Arthur amount to some of the finest moments of early 1980s punk.

In 1983, Morrison joined one of the finest versions of the Gun Club alongside Kid Congo Powers and Spencer P. Jones for a frenzied world tour that scurried from the U.K. to Australia, bringing a molten catalog of haunting, groundbreaking roots-punk tunes to the masses, like "Brother and Sister," the harried "Goodbye Johnny," and the much emulated "Sex Beat." With her trademark sculptural hair, opaque white face, and unmistakable beats, Morrison proved her sonic shape-shifting abilities. Clips from the Hacienda in Manchester reveal a band at the height of their career. Gun Club's sheer esoteric musicality—partly linked to Pierce's deep-seated fondness for blues, jazz, and Americana—made the band singularly transcendent.

Soon, Morrison graduated to the cryptic, somnambulist rock of Sisters of Mercy. By the mid-1980s, they were paragons of darkwave and Goth that wound up imprinting punk for subsequent years, including newcomers Alkaline Trio. The penetrating, solemn, and funereal ambience of the band, and singer Andrew Eldritch's heavy penchant for husky, dramatic crooning, was a perfect match for Morrison's brooding, insistent bass lines.

Like an imperishable figure withstanding all the varied directions of punk, she re-cast herself again, this time with the Damned, led by her husband, Dave Vanian, whom she wed in 1996. They released a blistering 'comeback' album, *Grave Disorder*, for Nitro Records (run by members of Offspring). Her elastic playing, and strong compositions by the crew, create rippling luster as the band tackles more literal subjects than ever, like the nature of politics ("Democracy") and the digital world's obsessive-compulsive magnetism ("Song.com").

Gone may be their early, dogged, ragged attempts of overturning rock'n'roll's inert mid-1970s overtures, but musically they deliver a tour-de-force. Yet the lyrics struck some as diluted and too of-the-moment rather than allegorical or universal. Live and loud, they presented no sign of decay on the tour with behemoths

White Zombie; unfortunately, their unquenchable vitality was not appreciated by the metal crowd multitudes. The tranquil bearing of Morrison, easily at home in the sinewy, pitched noise of the Damned's music, was uncanny, just as she had been in 1983 and 1978. Morrison always seemed uncontrived, tapping her iron-shod bass licks with tempered ease, as if she was a flagstone of measured fury. Though she has since retired, her musical impact is formidable. Her sheer cool-headedness, singular presence, and thatched involvement with year-zero punk, proto-hardcore, roots-punk, Goth punk, and resurrected 1976ers makes her an icon of untold vigor, keen ability, and seamless adaptability.

The VKTMs with Nyna Crawford

With a feral, outsider punk rigor, the VKTMs mounted a shock rock campaign that put them in league with bands like the Dwarves, Sluts for Hire, and Lunachicks. Never tame, and never abiding by any norms of good taste or by-the-book feminism, they could slip into a lusty song about little people ("Midget"), 'brainless' scenesters ("Hard Case"), gullible sex-repressed new wave boys ("Too Bad"), and over-drinking cheap booze ("Roma Rocket") just as easily as they could unleash a vendetta against the uber-wealthy ("God Damn the Rich").

As an imposing presence, politically incorrect Nyna Crawford captivated the crowds at joints like Mabuhay in San Francisco, venting into the mic with Lester Bangs/Wayne County

style bombastic anti-charm. From the late 1970s to early 1980s, they rankled audiences, stirred controversy, and executed a sardonic ribaldry, while still showing a soft spot for traditional rock'n'roll.

Their most pugnacious cuts like "White Girl" offer up a theater of anger and alienation, spite and spittle, of women trying to find their way in between communities and territories. They fight, are fought, and are thrown by birth into submission and castigated for shunning all manifestations of oppressors.

For a stellar tune, check out "Close But No Cigar" with its forceful choruses and preying bass lines, or the angst of "What's a Girl to Do," which pushes back with partly tongue-in-cheek vitriol at asshole, sex-obsessed men. After the untimely death of Crawford, the band has resurfaced over the last few years with barbed wire singer Sophie Vogel, who continues the band's onslaught with ease. But it was Crawford that cemented their legendary reputation.

Sonic Youth with Kim Gordon

Kim Gordon is the Michelangelo of experimental punk. Her musical landscape is hallowed ground. Unfettered by the world of hammy rock'n'roll clones, she made sonic sculpture from a cosmos of noise. She tore away the old definitions of bass playing: be the "anchor" of the band, be the robot-like metronome, be the quiet sidekick to the guitar, be the thick groove that remains passive, be the honey-voiced female back-up singer. Hell no.

Sonic Youth made the impossible happen by carving out a place for art-noise, especially the fire-eating, pornographic East Village transgressive era of

album, *Daydream Nation*. They transformed again as they appropriated portions of pop rock-accessibility into the album *Goo*, which catapulted them into "stardom," then took up D.C.-style renegade rage on *Dirty*. In fact, Ian MacKaye of Minor Threat, Fugazi, and others show up on "Youth Against Fascism." Through it all, Gordon was the one who signaled the true genius.

In the talk-rock distillation "My Friend Goo," Gordon surveys comic book saturated suburbia, including its fragmented wasteland, and creates an honest portrait of young America. In "Kool Thang," she reached back to stirring moments of soul music and classic country (the male-female call and response patterns) to shed light on the relationship between sexism and racism still raging today. On "Bull in the Heather" from *Experimental Jet Set, Trash, and No Star*, she seems to thumb through a personal diary and explore the psychology of relationships in nuanced, even surreal ways.

Other essential tunes include the spoken-word dreamscape of "Shadow of a Doubt," a former favorite of late-night 1980s MTV, and the intense critique of commodities on "The Sprawl," from *Daydream Nation*, all backed by the band's enigmatic un-rock. Even more recent fare like "Reena" and "What a Waste," both from the superb *Rather Ripped*, feature her trademark smarts ("you give me hollow stimulation"). For a revisited taste of updated 1980s Sonic Youth, try "Side2Side," from *NYC Ghosts and Flowers*, which feels as eerie, otherworldly, and poeticized as any of her work.

Trying to describe Kim Gordon in short form is like writing haiku about a deity. She was, and is, a musical suffragette that came, saw, and conquered. Her presence is felt deeply, widely, and profoundly.

Laughing Hyenas with Larissa Strickland

Strickland formed a dizzying, sometimes thunderous rhythmic section that molded epic albums like *You Can't Pray a Lie* and *Life of Crime*. The band was led by the torn-throat agonies of John Brannon, who has made an impactful reappearance in his much-worshipped, re-united hardcore band Negative Approach. In the Hyenas, though, Larissa Strickland and crew mustered up a Midwest cacophony that was heavily influenced by jazz musicians like Elvin Jones

and John Coltrane (listen to those drums on "Dedications to the One I Love.")

They were an uncanny presence, joining the ranks of bands like Tar, God Bullies, early Swans, and Cows, but they never quite fit the noise genre, partly due to the wheezy, ghostly journeys of Strickland's guitar or her fiery distorted wall-of-sound.

No carbon copy exists of them. They were sometimes red-eyed and rabid ("Black Eyed Susan"), and sometimes transfixingly damaged funk conveyors ("Lullaby and Goodnight") with howling emotional fits. *Life of Crime* is an epic achievement, bar none. It reveals deep, lacerating secrets about the human condition. "Everything I Want" cuts deep with a puncturing bass line and swings in huge strides as Strickland piles up notched infernos of distortion. Mid-paced "Hitman" is one of the closet cuts

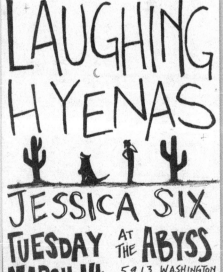

they ever made honoring simple rock'n'roll structures. "Let It Burn" comes close to the territory of early post-punks Killing Joke, albeit with a Detroit rock city center of gravity, "Kick" channels the swagger and dark poetry of Nick Cave (from Birthday Party), and the skittering, pulsing "Wild Heart" lets drum'n'bass ricochet against each other as Strickland lays down a curtain of white noise.

Sure, moments of later recordings like "Crawl" nod in the same direction, but soon the band was dispatched into the void. Larissa, who also sang for the pounding, new-wave drenched, pre-hardcore L-Seven in the early 1980s, died in the mid-2000s. But she remains undead in these recordings imbued with her singular chaos.

The Alley Cats with Dianne Chai

On the southern sides of Los Angeles, punk mobilized in incredible strides, sweeping bands like the Minutemen (San Pedro), Black Flag (Hermosa Beach), Descendents (Manhattan Beach), and Redd Kross (Hawthorne) into a collision with history. Yet, behind that wall of men (pierced every so often by the likes of Kira Roessler, Janet Housden, and others), came the urgent and uncanny alchemy of the Alley Cats. Their nimble bass player Diane Chai created a template for a pre/post hardcore sound that remains ever distinct, wiry, and powerfully cogent.

They simply never became part of the punk prairie fire on the same scale as their contemporaries. However, their scant recordings remain freshly scrubbed and transcendent. In fact, the likes of Bill Stevenson remain constant fans. He has told me how much they shaped the early sound of the Descendents, especially songs like "Cats' Limber," "Fluid," and rolling "Nothing Means Nothing Anymore." In the documentary film *Urgh: A Music War*, the Alley Cats can be seen tearing through an incredibly taut version of that tune with unstudied nonchalance.

Now mostly lost to faded history captured on grainy video, the Alley Cats feel more important than ever. Try their raucous, drum-powered theme "Just An Alley Cat," in which the calmness of Chai belies the full-throttled, searing, anthemic tune. It will stick to your ears like glue.

Here Holy Spain with Erica Guagliardi

Here Holy Spain is a much-overlooked but formidable gem from Dallas whose musical heaviness borrows a tint of stoner/desert rock and melds it effortlessly with mid-period Alkaline Trio, all throbbing to the core with the adept bass of Erica Guagliardi.

With a thunder-clapping, meaty, and somehow catchy-as-hell musical tour-de-force, Here Holy Spain keeps its punk tucked deep inside unbridled rock'n'roll riffage, like the Ramones married to Queens of Stone Age. Using Dallas as their vantage point, they roam the sonic hinterlands reclaiming head-banging: clean-cut, and likely with a whiff of Weezer, they show listeners that unkempt shaggy hair and arms chock-full of dodgy tattoos is not the only template. They are kin to a different trope.

If modern satellite radio can't find a place for the hurtlin' "Way Out One in Five," with its constant nitroglycerine drive, perfectly paced guitar breaks, switched-up speeds, and raspy then suddenly cloudy choruses, then radio is limp and used-up. The alliteration is piled high ("devout, devoid, and drowning," "see your senses sharp"), the rhythm leaves the listener with a kind of sonic motion sickness.

Percussive "Golden Gun" waxes in tough parallelism ("I feel . . . I cower . . . I never

Here Holy Spain, by David Ensminger

knew . . . ") about the bitterness that tends to gut people from the inside out. In fact, the storyline seems to infer the psyche of a loose-nut trigger man hitting breaking point and wanting the whole world to bleed with him. It's a compacted, fearsome piece of revenge poetry masked rock'n'roll vibes.

Meanwhile, "Hundreds of Heads Underwater" starts with a bit of bass and drum interplay until the floor tom beats the brats and the beachcore melodies sink in. Slower, exhaling frequently, and more loose than the rest of the EP, it feels like bubblegum rock with a bit of shrapnel stuck in to remind: this is music for the damned, not the sweet kids on the block.

Guagliardi continues her punk conquests in the damaged artcore of Lizzie Boredom, an all-female three-piece that recalls both Riot Grrrl's insistent, rough edges and late-1970s punk screech and flair.

The Avengers with Penelope Houston

Penelope Houston may have spent much of the last few decades as a painter, library archivist, and singer-songwriter chiseling smart, evocative tunes that would fit at any coffee shop, but in the late 1970s she was a trailblazer that sawed through the inertia of the "Me Generation" and furthered the eradication of gender norms first begun by pioneering feminists.

She was a soapbox hero with incredibly well-woven topical lyrics that underscored the fact that she was a seminal, incisive poet-punk. Even years later, unearthed/unreleased tunes like "The End of the World" (with the partially reformed band) are chilling, soaring powerhouses that sound like apocalyptic partners to their spare, momentous, and blood-curdling cover of the Rolling Stones "Paint it Black." Plus, check out Houston's remake of the band's religious dispatch "Corpus Christi" with Green Day's Billie Joe Armstrong on her solo album *Eighteen Stories Down* from 2003.

Very few bands have released such scant material and become such a huge part of the American punk idiom as the Avengers, who inspired everybody from Jello Biafra to Bikini Kill. Their singular, uncompromising vision made meaningful, muscular music for the heady days of San Francisco's late-1970s unrest, all under the sharp intelligence of Houston, who has bounced back every so often to reform the band and enthrall audiences all over again.

"Ask not what you can do for your country," she asks, slicing and dicing the words of John F. Kennedy, "What's your country been doing to you?" In the shadow of

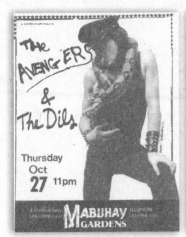

COINTELPRO and FBI probes, the right-wing tilt towards Ronald Reagan's vision of America, and a bitter legacy towards women, people of color, the Third World, and LGBTQ+ folks, the song remains a superheated mile marker of punk ideals. The band takes pop music's strut and remakes it with pogo possibilities and tireless two-minute wit.

War on Women with Shawna Potter and Nancy Hornburg

With blistering tunefulness that harkens back to the zenith hardcore days of Black Flag, Baltimore-based War on Women produced a confessional, contoured, and convulsive six-song EP called Improvised Weapons that remain their finest hour alongside their self-titled album. Although knee-deep in feminist creeds, don't expect mere socio-politico placards backdropped by assaulting, dark, and compressed musical templates. In contrast, they bury any sense of preachiness inside quickstep tunes that can be heavy enough to feel like an injection of lead into the backbone and nimble and acrobatic enough to satisfy any prog-punk fans. Examples include their stunning and short "Roe Vs. World," which outlines the true sensibilities of birth control, while "Let Your Voice Be Heard" works to break down down the silence surrounding rape.

Their track "Effemimania" aims to collapse binary gender norms. In cutting lyrics like "We all have a penis . . . We all have a clit," singer Shawna Potter offers up a "public cervix announcement" while shredding the notions that relationships should be defined by female "recipro-cunt" passivity and male-female antipodes. Sure, taken apart and deconstructed, the lines seem like heavy-duty philosophy for a song doused in such riffage, but the musical blitzkrieg and skill meld with theory-driven intelligence in tight-wound effectiveness.

"Broken Record" adds even darker shades of hypnotic guitar parts and spoken-word dialogues. War on Women subverts the male gaze. "What I'm wearing has only to do with the weather . . . I'm not your baby," snarls Potter when she is not re-enacting a pick-up scene on the corner, mimicking ignorant male pleas for phone numbers and attention. Impassioned and steadfast, the lyrics castigate male banter as "a broken record" as the song pushes back and forth with pummeling drums and fluctuating, powerhouse guitars.

To some degree, the band updates the Riot Grrrl intensity of Bikini Girl, but with Net-generation lacerating pithiness. Musically, the band sustains a cascading metallic dirge the whole time, mixed forcefully with abrupt and alluring tempo changes. Meanwhile, the songs' razor-slinging poetry avoids relying on tattooed punk clichés. To be sure, War on Women weave their vendetta-rock with tenacious talent and empowerment—it's a dark dance on the grave of misogynists and their enablers.

The Contractions

Too often both male and female journalists and academics have created a condescending, derisory "other" category for female punks. They are somehow treated as ambassadors of a naïve/incomplete/substandard style, as if they lack acute chops or know-how to compete onstage with boys trained from birth to wield guitars. Yet bands like the Contractions blow holes in that flimsy theory.

First and foremost, they are scrupulous, impeccable musicians steeped in punk spirit. They ignored genre games, boundaries, and rules, producing a dizzying blend that

is artful, articulate, and antsy. Listen to the insistent "No Questions," with its lean production values and acrobatic playing.

Meanwhile, the blistering mutant surf of "Pictures" (*Live at Lennon*) proves the percussive onslaughts of Debbie Hopkins are some of the best in the business, while "No Matter" beats hard and quick, but then throws down some elastic reggae-tinged bridges, giving the tune some swing and syncopation. And if you listen to the extra track from *SIR 1981*, you'll witness them plundering dub-funk, noise-riddled free jazz, and spoken word tirades.

Furthermore, bassist Kathy Peck is the C.O.F. of H.E.A.R. Foundation—Hearing Education and Awareness for Rockers, which "has redefined the tools, language, and image surrounding hearing loss prevention both in San Francisco and around the world, attracting support and partnerships with high profile recording artists, health organizations, and media-enriched museums and concert events."

Plus, she is one hell of a storyteller, which became an invaluable asset to the (un)oral history of the Deaf Club I assembled for *Maximum RocknRoll*, which was then reprinted in my book *Left of the Dial*. As she described the Deaf Club:

"The place was filthy. My boots would stick to the floor. The deaf people would dance to the vibration of the beat. Robert Hanrahan would do a radio show with Johnny Walker (BBC punk rock DJ) on the side of the stage, it seems. Robert Hanrahan, manager of The Offs, discovered the San Francisco Club for the Deaf in 1978, and was able to rent it on a nightly basis. It was great fun. The Deaf Club was more like a neighborhood place, very underground, in the Mission District. People would give the deaf sign for a beer as The Offs, The Contractions, Middle Class, No Alternative, and the Dils played. People like Ginger Coyote (*Punk Globe*) would hang out, dance, and drink. The bathroom was full of graffiti. We'd load in, and the punk boys' bands would always get in crazy fights—Brittley Black, drummer of Crime, fell out of the upstairs window many a night. The deaf people were receptive. They could 'hear' through the wooden floor—a simple floor, made from planks or linoleum. It could catch the vibrations. Frank Moore from the Outrageous Beauty Pageant was there in his wheelchair that people dragged upstairs, since it was on the second floor. Dirk Dirksen (Mabuhay club promoter and San Francisco music icon) nurtured his career."

Tribe 8

Though the millennial generation has been waging a cultural war concerning LGBTQ+ issues, a whole era of outpunk/queercore seems to have been brushed to the side, particularly dyke punk, whose singer Lynn Breedlove bulldozed 'haters' with relentless, unrepentant, cheeky glee. Tribe 8 helped pave the path that most kids now take for granted, including a million smudged tattoos (once the domain of sideshow freaks, sailors, bikers, and junkies), androgyny/gender-bending galore, rogue backdoor taboo sexuality, and butch-femme escapades.

Multiracial and musically endowed, Tribe 8 stirred the pot fiercely and risked everything for their beliefs. In doing so, they often perturbed the nightcrawler punk legions as much as live-by-day normals. In their queer/lez glory, Tribe 8 pounced on lame suburbanites causing "Lezbophobia," while painting an uproarious portrait of punk-as-fuck gals turning "femme in the streets" in the tune "Butch in the Streets."

They advocated for the body modification nation on "People Hate Me," a hardcore chunk of protest against those who demeaned punk's unruly bodies decades after Londoners poked holes in their cheeks with baby pins. "Wrong Bathroom" attacks the dismal logic of binary bathrooms with comic precision, the daily conundrums of queer non-conformity, and the wide-eyed confusion of everyday gas station Middle America trying to grasp what has happened to sex/body norms.

In creating their hodgepodge of acid-metal deconstruction, anger-stoked punk tirades, dyke bar drunken paradise, and jazzy-ska monstrosity, they paint a lurid picture of a lost and shunted San Francisco now painted over by gentrification. Assimilation and normalization may feel like freedom to some, but to others, the gay/queer/dyke ghettos—the ones drawn in masterful musical strokes by the tasteless onslaughts of the crew of Tribe 8—feel ever more patently authentic, transgressive, and subcultural. They like their music porn dirty.

Babes in Toyland

From the northern murk of winter midnight Minneapolis came the sheer abrasion of Babes in Toyland. They seemed to behead all the outdated, remaining notions of backwards-looking female norms in the years marking the third dizzying decade of sweltering punk. Just as next-door neighbors Prince and even Husker Du challenged funk and punk sexualities and added fuel to the fight against strict status quo conventions by bending the rules here and there, Babes in Toyland, led by Kat Bjelland, upended female-relegated good manners, passivity and restraint, and cleanliness-is-Godliness rituals still clinging on in the Bush years.

They replaced those restrictive qualities with a free-roaming, uncontrolled female sense of antagonism. The "grotesque" body becomes a site of contention where all decorum breaks down. Inhibitions are swept aside by a codex for living uninhibited, gnarly, and free. On tunes like "Swamp Pussy" and "Vomit Heart," androgyny is

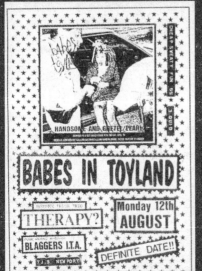

drawn in blood. So, if Hole and L7 seemed a bit too methodical and mainstream, Babes in Toyland were looser, unfettered, and tumultuous, competing with bands on the local label Amphetamine Reptile for sheer decibels, dark guttural weirdness, and genre-imploding idiosyncrasy.

While the Top 40 world immersed in the pretty persuasions of goopy good girl Amy Grant pining for love, the underground world fervently bathed in the sometimes garbled, bitterness, and anguish of these tunes. Such tunes force listeners to grasp the (un)pretty reality of punk. Miniskirts, flowery dresses, and tiny red bows worn in videos like "Bruise Violent" add irony and a disjointed vibe to the feeding frenzy as the band holds such symbols, visual tropes, and lady gear hostage.

By the end, the band used smeared make-up and roaming motorcycles as their nods to street-wise counterculture, which they remade in the era first inaugurated by Lydia Lunch and Frightwig, then contoured by their own counterparts like Tragic Mulatto, Lunachicks, and Tribe 8. All such bands were a potent fungicide trying to rid the world of abject boy-rule and pretty girl repression and sameness.

Fabulous Disaster

Fabulous Disaster was led by Lynda Mandolyn, who also played with the female power trio Inside Out in the Midwest. They earned a spot in the Detroit Music Awards Hall of Fame in 1993 and reunited in 2012. Together with the Eyeliners, Fabulous Disaster formulated a melodic punk-pop plan that evoked a musical terrain somewhere between smart, teen-frenzied comics like *Love and Rockets*, the spiky attitudes and gritted teeth of bands like Snap-Her, and the carnal, wise-crackin' deluge pop of the Dickies. Quick tunes like "Minimize My Faith" balanced sweet cheerleader charm with cutthroat kid toughness.

Though the band should have easily slid aside bands like Green Day and Alkaline Trio, they never seemed to reach the masses, perhaps because they were an all-girl unit outflanked by the Donnas. Back then only so much oxygen existed in a room for girl bands. Or maybe they were not a "pretty girl" squad. They were a tattooed, mixed-sexuality, lewd-leaning, kick-ass tribe that became a bit too dangerous for a typical Johnny or Joey. "I like to play with fire," they howl on "My Static." Meanwhile, as the crushing tom-tom interplay lays down the rhythm for "Crush," the narrator feels "tangled in knots . . . " and ready to shut it down and "crash and burn." Such tunes unleash a violent-tinged pathos for the punk inside us all.

They were impeccable tunesmiths that produced devious songs that were tight, unmannered, snotty around the edges, and never drifting towards pompousness or perkiness. Because of that, they always felt in command of a musicscape that leveled the playing field by exposing anger, bitterness, woe, and confusion that smears the hearts of both sexes.

Here is a portion of an exchange we had in *Left of the Dial*.

LOTD: You have said that, "Some days I feel that being all female may keep us from becoming what we could be, as big as we could be, because we all know it's a man's world." So is there a glass ceiling in the music world?

Sally: Yeah, totally.

Lynda: I've said this before in interviews. People have a misconception about girl bands. The big thing that we get is people coming up and saying, "You know I really don't like female bands, I don't like girl bands, but after I saw you guys, it changed everything." I don't think they see us as a girl band, they see us as rocking out, which is what we do. I think we change a lot of minds when people see us live.

Sally: We have to prove ourselves . . .

Lynda: Night after night.

Sally: Every single night people come to the show and totally basically walk by our merch and don't even really look at it, and then after we play, they're like, wow, I can't believe it. They just come in thinking it's just another girl band, I don't care, so we totally have to prove ourselves every night.

Lynda: We do, and that's fine.

Sally: Which I don't think guy bands have to do.

LOTD: But do bands like the Donnas appearing on *Saturday Night Live* and the Distillers going on tour with No Doubt, or Sleater Kinney on tour with Pearl Jam, make it easier or make it harder?

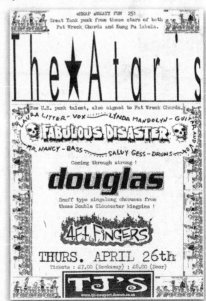

Lynda: Hopefully, it will open the doors for more all-female bands to get signed and move up one step up. I've said this in interviews too, but what is the last time you heard of a girl band that wrote their own music, played their own instruments . . .

LOTD: Is that a stab at the Donnas?

Lynda: No! The Go Go's . . . are a big influence on us. I saw that and said, that's what I want to do, I want to be in a girl band and do that. What do girls, or young people in general, what do they have to look up, Britney Spears and all this other crap. I am very happy for the Donnas.

LOTD: You have a nephew who liked them and you referred to his favorite band as the Backdoor Boys . . .

Lynda: Actually it was my niece. But guys like Jack Grisham from TSOL has a thirteen year old daughter, so if his kids want to be rebellious would they go to a reformed Adolescents show or a Britney Spears concert?

Sally: I don't think that buying Britney Spears is being rebelling though. It's so commercially acceptable by everyone, so if you are going with something commercially acceptable, you are not being rebellious really. It would probably be more rebellious to be into something like rockabilly or something.

Lynda: You never know. My friend's stepson was raised on punk rock, and he screamed in punk rock bands when he was four and five years old and now he is out buying rap records, and he is fifteen.

LOTD: So, it depends. Is that disappointing to you?

Lynda: Well, yeah, and it also shows that he is probably going through a phase. Like my niece. She liked Brittney Spears and all this other stuff, now she loves Fabulous Disaster, NOFX, and Good Charlotte. She's into punk rock now, so I am happy.

The B-52s with Kate Pierson and Cindy Wilson

As I eagerly and wholeheartedly attest, The B-52s (with the ingenious multi-instrumental Kate Pierson and Cindy Wilson) were punks who combined rave-worthy music, an attack of the killer bouffants (which should be the title of their memoir!), and endless lightheartedness while they deconstructed pop culture. In doing so, they managed to make sonic collages worthy of museum exhibits. Where else do hog-wild beatnik bongos meet B-movie science fiction ("Planet Claire")?

BENEFIT FOR THE
NATIONAL AUDUBON SOCIETY
"THE BIRDS AND THE B'S"...

the
B-52's

NEW LP MESOPOTAMIA
ON WARNER BROS...

WITH...

THE JUDYS

MON. MARCH 1
8:00PM
MUSIC HALL

TICKETS AVAILABLE at all TICKETMASTER LOCATIONS

They also made a huge impact on late 1990s/2000s punk, post-punk, and post-hardcore, from Sleater Kinney and Retisonic to many others. Listen to their 1978-80 live videos and audio for their raw glee. The breathlessly catchy "Devil in My Car" and "Private Idaho" are two of their most dizzying cuts. They utterly reek with three-way vocal tantrums and manic harmonies, like "Beware of the gate," "watch out for signs," and don't be blind to the "awful surprise," as well as their final admission, "I'm goin' to Hell in my old Chevrolet." These tunes juxtapose sheer punk pluckiness with limber new wave grooves.

Unbelievably, they gestated in Georgia, but their amalgam of spy'n'surf musical slyness and mondo B-movie feel is anything but humid southern belle terrain. Skip the sweet tea and mint julep—grab a glow-in-the-dark hula hoop, aerosol cans for enlarged chemical-induced mounds of hair, and orange cat-rim glasses instead!

Their hit song, "Rock Lobster," is a a 6-minute barrage of giant crustaceans, all foregrounded by shrill never-ending vocal warbling (imagine a human songbird on acid), synth blasts, meaty beats, and torso-twisting yelps. "Lava" is all about pent-up action, hormones, and lust, all while simultaneously threaded with Tiki party apocalypse imagery ("crackin' like a Krakatoa!"). All in all, through electric voltage, they offer Dayglo dance party beach themes for the concrete jungle—all hitched to their 'pleasure forever' operator's manual.

The Kills and Discount with Alison Mosshart

Before becoming a sixteen-year stalwart of electro-blues, dark-alt rock, and post-punk idol as one half of the suave duo the Kills (think June and Johnny Cash for the brave new world), Alison Mosshart made successive waves in Discount, who tore away the best part of emo punk habits (sincerity and ennui rolled into folds) and added layers of throbbing, guitar-heavy pop and socio-cultural observations.

The Kills have perfected a sexy, cool-to-the-touch fusion—their reductionist methods work well with their mixology—a song-style shot glass of Heavy Trash thrown in here, and a Raveonettes cocktail punk glamour etched into the grooves over there. There are echoes of the Gossip's beguiling trademark force exhibited in tunes like the Kills' dance-floor-sequence, smoky-voiced, yearning "Hard Habit to Break." While "Siberian Nights" offers seductive pulsebeats, smokehouse bluesy asides, and whispery lipstick allure, forming an intoxicating, inviting aural drug in the hips (if your joints don't loosen, you ears aren't working).

Mosshart's singing in Discount was higher-pitched, earnest as voices between string strung soup can telephones, and noticeably less lacquered. In turn, she invoked youthful personal pleas and touted metaphors as easy as loose change ("it's raining on the other side of these walls / the thunder reminds us of times when we hoped for nothing but storms"). In these tender, but smart-as-hell years, she had an incredible hold on surefire language gymnastics, like "Half Fiction" ("there is distance more than

Photos by Ken Blaze, 1997, Cleveland, OH Speak in Tongues

miles/but our ideas are adjoining canals"), which observes the inherent distance cast even in the closest relationships.

Then their achingly mature *Crash Diagnostic* (2000's breakout album) stoked the same sensibilities even further; even a fragment of the lyrics reads like flash fiction, such as "Math Won't Miss You" ("scrub all the carpets/turn over the mattress/burn all the outfits/draw drape the windows") capture the heart of dissatisfaction in pure imagery. The soaring cut "Broken to Blue" takes the grand prize: it musters a neo-Fugazi (think *Repeater*) propulsion and a personal call to mission ("it's a fragile world we're standing on") without being plainly, or painfully, obvious and histrionic.

Others adore the band's EP of Billy Bragg covers ("Great Leap Forward," etc.), the speed-infused, let's-bust-through-the-confusion and overcome the letdown years of "Am I Missing Something," the slower tidal wave of "Pocket Bomb," the slightly abstract analysis of domestic disrepair in "Toxic House," or their gruffer fare, including "On the Tracks," which drills musically along the vein of the hectic-paced, duct-taped together, mid-period, emotional salvos akin to Jawbreaker.

Discount suffered by insisting to only work with a single record label for their entire tensure—albeit one that changed names with every album. And it promptly fell apart as label proprieter Tim Lyman suffered from Crohn's Disease and Discount promptly broke up after the departure of two original members.

Some might not be able to reconcile the two worlds of Mosshart, but they offer portraits of an artist living through three decades of musical honesty—each bracing, each aligned to the truth of the times: crackerjack youthful verve meets cunning, but never cloying, adult gestalt.

The Lewd and VS. with Olga de Volga

The Lewd were a kind of American broken dream machine, spewing songs about abandoned babies, killing oneself, mobile homes, and the overall climate of fear like roving reporters chasing the grit of daily life in the late-industrial collapse called America. For a short stint, fetish leather leader Olga de Volga (Texas-born Susan Smith) joined them in her post-Offs and post-VS. days. As singer J. Sats/Satz Baret/Beret stated to *Punk Globe*, she "never played by the rules/always fought against the tide." Her outfits alone were shows of power—stark Nordic hair sometimes infused with bold swathes of iridescent color, motorcycle boots (not just pretend garb—she was a roving biker who worked as a funeral escort), bandanas tightened around her neck, and studded armbands at the ready.

The Lewd were a feral bunch—rhythmically akin to DOA and the Subhumans, matching the hooks and frenzy of the Germs in their twilight, and they had one foot planted in the thrilling guitar stampede of the Dead Boys and Iggy Pop ("I Got A Right" period). As raucous, heavy hitters, they unleashed a mercilessness sardonic sneer that skewered both lowlife America, outlined the politics of fear and repression (often masking as suburban normality in the parent-teacher-cop-military nexus), and marauded with weaponized punk insolence (via trash can drums and browbeating guitars).

Thus, they became restless parasites from underground America trying to unsettle the judges and juries. They brewed a dark wit the Sex Pistols should have envied. Olga was totally in her element, in the eye of a miscreant musical storm, with agile fluid chops, but then she was gone—first, to step into the Undead, then into faraway Hawaii. But her rabid glow remains in these tunes.

Carla /Karla 'Mad Dog /Maddog' Duplantier

Duplantier, a New Yorker transplant to Los Angeles, worked for the postal office and first heard punk rock via the show Rodney on the Roq (radio station KROQ FM), who spun the Ramones' "Sheena is a Punk Rocker" in 1977, which she promptly bought at Bomp Records—store, fanzine, and record label of local heroes like the Weirdos and Germs. A longtime skateboarder and drummer, she quickly learned songs by Blondie and Dead Boys and befriended Kira Roessler (future member of Sexsick with Mad Dog and Black Flag bass player).

Seeing shows by West Coast legends like the Skulls and Avengers, she became a resident rocker at the Hollywood club The Masque, and joined the Controllers, who released the EP "Suburban Suicide" (Siamese, 1979) with her behind the kit. Their tunes are an abrasive, grinding, and degenerate wallop of rock'n'roll, indebted to the likes of the Dogs and Stooges.

Other cuts like their drinking-binge folk ditty bastardization "Barnacle Bill the Sailor," thunderous surf wreckage "Do the Uganda" (hey, let's sadistically and sardonically attack African madmen dictators!), and "White Trash Christ" prove their riotous brand of rock'n'roll avoided any predictable tedium and restraint—they were true brawling bards of bad taste. "Slow Boy," with a neo-hardcore pace and snot for limber lube, showcases the complete control of Mad Dog on the drumset: she hurtles through the song with total ease, ramping up the rhythm with indelible skill.

Throughout the years, she played with the .45s, Legal Weapon, El Rey, and Leaving Trains, but during the 1980s, she also rooted herself in England. She first played in the band Precious Few and later joined Jimmy the Hoover. Having opened for Bow Wow Wow, they were first signed by Innervision, a label affiliated with CBS, where they released the single "Tantalise" and reached the hit charts in 1983, which led to two appearances on Top of the Pops.

In the 1990s, returning to work with Kidd Spike, she further proved her monumental abilities in Skull Control. She is completely unhinged behind the kit, turning "Radio Danger" into a potent maelstrom. Many vintage tunes re-emerge, like "Suburban Suicide," but the production is top notch this time, and Mad Dog is completely in her element—a wizard of timing, fills, and velocity. And the humor is still relentless, as the pummeling "Smells Like Bad Nirvana" (which lifts portions of "Life of Crime" from the Weirdos) attests.

As a pioneering black punk who challenged both the color codes and the masculinity usually enshrined behind drum sets, she set a whole new standard for resistance, musicianship, and resilience.

Melt Banana with Yasuko O.

Few artists can render postmodern pastiche music so unfathomable and accessible at the same time. Like Japanese counterparts the Boredoms and Ruins, Melt Banana seem to occupy a genre-free zone, a world without stiff musical borders, in which super-intense, elastic extreme music is the norm. By combining tropes and traits of genres like powerviolence, D-beat, and screamo with the worlds of techno-metal, avant-gardism, and tone poem bursts, plus exhibitions of sheer noise, they are the very essence of brash. They attract masterminds like engineers extraordinaire Steve Albini, of Shellac fame, and Jim O'Rourke, who has worked with Sonic Youth and Stereolab.

"Shield for Your Eyes, A Beast in the Well on Your Hand" is a primer for their whole catalog. It is a zealous, well-coordinated, total assault that combines mosh metal breakdowns, supersonic speed in sections, and a limber agility to hammer out rhythmic changes in perfect ease. Yasuko's singing, like dizzying gymnastics, intersects the mayhem with perfect ease.

Their alliterative lyrical wordplay is often wonky and tantalizing, as can be seen in "Candy Gun": "Keep out the careful cats / Can I wake a sweeper setoff?" The song first surfaces like an ambient soundtrack, replete with shoreline water mumbles and soft guitar sculpture that gives way to contemporary post-thrash urges. It's breathless, transcendent, and scaled up. The careening, multiple time signatures of "The Hive" are equally brutal,

friday 13th gilman st.
SPAZZ
MELT BANANA
TION ... AN CREEPS
HUMAN VAN CREEPS ON
THERMA CANDY
MEDICATION TIME

Satanic human sacrifices are a slap in God's face.

.625 flyer
.625 flyer

making contemporary noise-makers seem like easy listening "Lefty Dog (Run, Caper, Run)" is thrash metal for digital anarchists—if you ever needed something to wake up your entire neighborhood at 4 A.M., this would out-maneuver most grindcore. While are always an innovative force, they also show some allegiance to past idols, like their deconstructed, mixed-genre take on "Uncontrollable Urge" by Devo (is this nutso bubblegum-metal-funk-punk?) and hard-syncopating tweak-the-hip "Sweeper." They take these iconic grooves and inject a fierce, weird allure and video game super-blast tenacity.

"Grave in the Hole (Pitfall Fits a Bit)" reminds me of Crass' noisiest abstract moments, taken to d-beat extremes. Meanwhile, "Spider Snipe" comes close to heroic rock'n'roll tirades. Their shape-shifting, manic unhinged exploits, indelible twist'n'turn annihilation beats, and outré musical outbursts offer balance and vision, including revolutionary ruckus and madly honed craft.

Fire Party

As Revolution Summer faded and bands on Dischord Records, the lauded label from Washington D.C., took new paths in the post-hardcore era, Fire Party helped define the gestalt and the power of the scene. In doing so, they joined the likes of mid-period Scream as well as Fidelity Jones,

Amy Pickering and Skeeter Thompson (Scream), Tulsa, 2015, by David Ensminger

Shudder to Think, and 3 to show how punk's earnestness, guitar-thronged maturity, and sense of abstract poetics, which paved the way for Jawbox, could enthrall. While not as heavy and metallish as all-female powerhouse L7, Fire Party could nonetheless grind with a groove, anchored by the rollicking bass of Kate Samworth and powerful drumming of Nicky Thomas on tunes like "Make It Quick."

Plus, the vocals of singer Amy Pickering could shift, within seconds, from a mellow lull to a shattering shriek. At her fiercest, on tracks like "Bite," she whips up a kind of punk Janis Joplin, though the blues swagger is transformed into punk insistence. "Just bite it off and chew your way through," she cajoles with throat-burning, raspy intensity. Musical moments of "First Course" feel faintly like Joy Division. Just listen to the spare, all-alone drums at the end, which are enforced by the quintessential feeling of emptiness, uncertainty, and purposelessness.

Yet, the unapologetic guts and stamina embedded in Pickering's voice proves that the reason people sing about gray modes is to actually reinforce the will to live. One must taste a bit of the void, the strain of feeling at wit's end, in order to understand how to settle back into the arms of life and be smarter, bolder.

"I don't want to hide any longer behind anger and pain," she sings on "Prisoner," easily one of their toughest cuts, which plows ahead as Pickering deconstructs the nature of living in public, full and honest. It is a relentless barn burner. The same might be said for "Only Nine Mottos," a two-minute torch that is self-reflexive and a bit meta-critical: Pickering tackles songwriting itself, all while recognizing that often ". . . first comprehension isn't what frees."

Perhaps it's more like the act of seeing and re-seeing, writing and rewriting; meanwhile, the very act of writing about music, the sometimes wanna-be intellectual efforts of people like me, may be like turning an artist "inside out . . . then we can see what's really me." Perhaps

that offers pure irony. Reviewers think they can shine a transparent light on writers, but the actual slippery sense of self, the shifting person behind the song, will always be elusive. Words fail to deliver certainty, alas, on both sides of the process.

Above the band's throbbing din, its weaving and tilting rock'n'roll sensibilities, and its soluble intensity, Pickering is the poet at the heart of it all. She seems to reach out to poet Rainer Maria Rilke on "Engine," search for modes of control and contentment on "Cake," tear apart the notion of luck and desire on "Basis," and deal with the compulsive, omnivorous need for space and breathing room on "Drowning Intentions." That tune seems to suggest that the walls people construct, keep them negotiating how much they are willing to share, perhaps suffer, as people impose their wills (even in kindness) upon each other. These tendencies end up molding relationships that never quite satisfy. In the end, perhaps all people have is an unstable image of each other. Luckily, the music is a well-shaped maelstrom that keeps all these thoughts from being too ponderous. Pickering is at the helm, the guide to an inner-country, never flummoxed to a point of paralysis. Freedom is always ticking under her breaths, and still is, for she has become a fervid outdoor climber, hiker, and photographer, always seeking the lone, difficult stretches that make life seem more spontaneous, spirited, and worthwhile.

Crass with Eve Libertine and Joy De Vivre

*P*enis Envy by Crass is a stupendous slice of emancipatory outreach, a treatise of punk intelligentsia in motion, and a gendered form of combat rock to waken the sleeping feminist inside all of us. If the first records by the band were audacious, choleric, brutally-fast polemics that struck right as punk had been neutered by major record labels, this work is like a volume of insurrection with concept-rock variation that will always be relevant.

The album is partly shaped, shaded, and defined by the thin-as-a-wire production values—in which each instrument sounds isolated in an operating room—and the manic jazz-punk drums of clever, dexterous Penny Rimbaud. The twin engine vocal deliveries of Eve Libertine and Joy De Vivre are incisive, theoretically inclined, but still glued to punk angst. Altogether, the album is a devastating attack on all things Western. As they stake the moral high ground and draw lines between confusion and control, they create the essential Crass myth. This was a band less concerned with brazen power chord pyrotechnics and far more inclined to deconstruct the very essence of rock'n'roll rebellion.

"Poison In Pretty Pill" attacks the outmoded notion of manicured beauty, "tactile lies of glaze and gauze," that masks the wounds behind looking perfect in a scarred world. In an uncanny poetry of anger and outrage, they nimbly draw links between the advertisements brimming with dishonest layers of falsehood and the mashed wounds of a war zone ringed by barbed wire fences. "What the Fuck?" tries to trace the cobwebs of crimes that lead to the destruction of the earth, in which women become the synecdoche, a symbol of the whole imbalance. Unchecked destructive

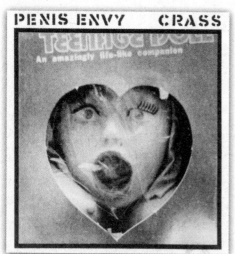

lust wreaks havoc on lands and bodies, and any craven response is repugnant. Don't be timid, they proclaim, because that means sharing duties in the basic plot-line: the deprivation and debasement of others. In some ways, the tune is the closest cousin to the counter-cultural 1960s, for they end the song with a potent sense of "breath, light, life, and *peace!*" that stands in dire contrast to the world of patriarchal chaos.

Throughout their music they dissect the domestic sphere, and language itself, as jail cells. Men dub women as "goddesses, mothers, and whores," and these simpering oversimplifications de-humanize them, just as rings on women's fingers chain them to a "packed and ready" life of suppression. Equally disdained is the incarceration of romance, the plague of modern times, propelled by "magazines, the cinema, and the glossy shops," which add layers and layers of naturalized normative behavior that justify "tokens of possession."

If ever an album linked the work of early feminists and anarchists like Emma Goldman with the peak years of punk's promise, this is it. In fact, the distance and time between the eras seems to meld as their theories merged in the sound of this onslaught, which forever shaped discourse in punk.

Eve Libertine still works in contentious, conceptual formats, like "Listen, Little Man!," an avant-garde sound opera made using "voice, test tone generators, and video," inspired by the work of psychoanalyst Wilhelm Reich. Hence, her spirit remains alive and well, unrestrained and undaunted. Crass is simply one document of her untrammeled dedication to art.

The Kimonos with Gina Miller

Hailing from the steamy nights of Houston, TX, The Kimonos plied their musical trade with toughened verve, offering 'dark wave' meets aggressive 'post-punk' imbued with prowess and panache. Though adored in the seething Texas underground for their profuse sweat'n'power live shows, they remained under the radar, honing songs rooted in razor smarts and nimble musicality. The members' previous bands—including Magnetic 4, Causey Way, Japanic, and The Scaries—toured the U.S.A. and Europe after releasing lauded material, prepping the grounds for The Kimonos' assault.

Combining hints of the Yeah Yeahs Yeahs and Glass Candy with homegrown abandon, including layers of sonic new wave shrapnel tucked into noir aesthetic, titanic tunes like "Cataclysmo" create a vibe of late-night, scary seduction that singer Gina Miller and Ken Shoen pucker up and deliver with deadly earnestness. The track evokes suspense, seedy intoxication, and a panoramic distorted cinema of sound that melds the guitar lines of eerie Dead Kennedys tracks with the formidable Devo-deconstructed thrust of Servotron. The result is a mash-up style, a bustling and bristling hybrid, that feels taut and tangy, melting down ineffectual and milquetoast pretenders in its wake.

The Kimonos, Houston, by David Ensminger

"Side by Side" recalls a mid-1990s era of alt-rock headiness, including thorny, Pixies-esque guitar patterns. The co-ed vocals banter, weave, and duck, keeping a core pop power intact. The pop tendencies of The Kimonos feel tempered by nausea and pain, letting listeners fly through pointed and brutally honest emotional tumult in mere minutes.

In all, the Kimonos embodied a fractured and fomented sense of post-punk, but they don't truss it up with mimicry. They offer up, instead, a rough cut painting of their own, defined by a steady diet of good taste and nimble musicianship. Where most bands end up klutzy and schmaltzy, the Kimonos were taste-makers with a genius knack for reinventing and redefining.

Gina Miller

Before I even existed, music was shaping my life. It is rumored my parents heard each other singing back and forth and fell in love with each others' voices before they actually met in Mexico, where their respective families lived next door to one another. My mom was a mariachi singer in the 1970s and sang up until the time of her death. She sang all the time, and I grew to love the R&B ladies I overheard: Aretha, Tina Turner, Shirelles, Diana Ross, etc. Along with that, our entire family would get together almost every weekend, and mom and her seven siblings would take turns playing guitar and singing old Mexican ballads.

At about 15, I started hanging out with the 'outsider' crowd, the gothic girls that turned me on to new wave, ska, and punk—The Cure, Morrissey, Joy Division, Blondie. I moved back to Houston, a huge metropolis to me, and music became an easy 'in' to connect with the skater boys and the cool punk kids. In high school, I learned a hard lesson in peer cruelty and discarded my more naïve side for the hard edged "punk rock/take no shit" persona, gaining more influence by Kathleen Hanna and other underground feminist movement artists and zines like Bitch and Bust. Locally, I loved Mydolls, Pain Teens, SugarShack, DeSchmog and Stinkerbell.

Fusing everything I loved, I landed singing somewhere in the middle as the "last resort" choice for the surf/garage rock band, The Magnetic IV. My bandmate/then-fiancee who formed the band had put out a call for a singer, and not a single person responded, so he finally asked me if I would do it. Back in the earliest days of practice, I was scared to death to sing in front of anyone, so I wouldn't even face the band during rehearsals.

I made fast friends of the ladies—learning to stick together in a somewhat misogynistic scene, guys outnumbered us musicians at least five to one. I leaned on folks like DJ Rosa Guerrero, London Girl, Junior Varsity, Gun Crazy, Zipperneck, Japanic, and those who we played with/supported on tour like the Regrettes, the Bad Apples, the BellRays, the Tuna Helpers, and the Jewws.

The Kimonos, Rudyards, Houston, by David Ensminger

At our first show, I was heckled by a member of Rusted Shut, "Show me your tits!" somehow, before I could process how mortified I was, I yelled back, "I thought I told you to wait in the car!" During soundcheck at the Engine Room, the sound guy asked me if I was as loud as I was soundchecking and only half-joked, "Yeah girls shouldn't even be allowed on a mic." I felt creeped out by people ogling me onstage, even my own bandmate once commented, "Your ass looks really good in that skirt." (I never wore it again). I tried to take back my personal power through *more* aggression—wearing sunglasses, so I didn't have to make eye contact and sometimes flicking lit cigarettes into the air. I even once got nominated for best vocalist in our local weekly. When I inquired why the band wasn't asked to play in the awards showcase, I was told, "Vocals aren't a *real* instrument." I can't count the number of times I was mistaken for being a roadie/groupie/girlfriend of one of the guys in my band.

When we formed The Kimonos, I was relieved that most of the focus was off of me and onto the mania of our frontman/guitarist. I grew as a singer—and even tackled the vocal stylings of my idol, Deborah Harry, with our covers project called Mexican Blonde. The biggest compliment I've gotten was about a month away from my son's birth, where I ditched my heels onstage and fell to my knees while still playing the keyboard with one hand and my mic in the other. A friend said he'd never seen the gospel rocked barefoot and pregnant.

I ended up working in the music business legitimately, doing PR work for SugarHill Studios, and produced the video webcast, *Live From SugarHill*, to help promote so many talented and emerging artists from my hometown. I helped to coordinate efforts for the first iteration of Girls Rock Camp Houston, even though I wasn't able to take a larger role in the organization. I served a four year term on the board of the GRAMMY organization before leaving the arts/culture/tech industry altogether to pursue my passion. Now I incorporate music as a tool to guide students through their yoga practices. Even though I am not in a band fulltime, you may catch me onstage for the occasional benefit/reunion show and definitely in the crowd to support local and touring acts.

Iowa Beef Experience with Simone Rinehart

Their "Trailer Park" single contained bits of beef jerky stuck down in the plastic sleeve. The sludgy behemoth was produced by Steve Albini from Shellac and Big Black. It offers a dense, meaty, murky, and chunky sound. Side A is right up the alley of other acid-punk noiseniks, though bringing a more heavy-footed approach.

They deliver herky-jerky rhythms and bastardized, defoliated, sandpaper-burnished vocals, anchored by bass player Simone Rinehart. Side B's tongue-breaking song titled "Dope Smoking Rednecks from Cedar Rapids Trapped in an Alternative Reality" is woven with more Black-Sabbath-style heavy thunder groove, which quickly gives way to metallic, double-bass drum, and an up-tempo mayhem that would not have been unwelcome at the local trailer park dive bar. Perhaps the best feature is the artwork: imagine grotesque, two-color, hillbilly psychedelia. This is haunting, Neanderthal stuff from the bowels of Iowa City.

Meanwhile, the album *Personalien* continues the weird, murky madness: enmeshed noise and cathartic horror seem to intertwine effortlessly on pummeling tunes like "Hardcore Fan." The drums are scaled up, careening and dizzying on "Making the Monster A Snack," which is every bit as trad-minded as a lo-fi Led Zeppelin wanna-be bar band, if the band was strung out on highgrade barbiturates, watched too many zombie movies, and chose to freak out everybody at the bar.

Few "noise" bands ever really lived up to the moniker, either in terms of genre, pretense, or attitude. But in this band's hands, the noise repertoire on tunes like "Tools of the Trade" is palpable, intense, grueling, phantasmagoric, and aberrant. "Love Muscle #96" shows off their musical punches too, like hideously mutant jazz-metal that shows deep, sly tendencies hinting at a musical intelligence and interplay festering deep in its bowels.

The band evokes seriously seminal, bizarro Midwest fare, but Rinehart is anything but a country bumpkin—she plows and weaves, syncopates with fierceness, wrings the bass like a mop, and infuses the whole attack with underlying twists. Check out "Nonstop Nacho" to see her at her height.

Dinah Cancer of Castration Squad, Vox Pop, 45 Grave

45 Grave were colossal textbook examples of the horror-rock genre—campy, dramatized icons for lurid nightbreeders that weaved heavy rock'n'roll panache with bastardized punk. "Party Time" was their bona fide anthem that mixed a gruesome tale of child abuse and family degradation with exhortations of party time—the sound of the tormentor's dark glee. That is enough to make anyone cringe and mosh at the same time.

Though often shrugged off as guitar-heavy novelty punk, 45 Grave in the 1980s was quite nuanced. They amassed a musical arsenal that put them far above the chicanery of most metal-punk hybrids. Plus, in terms of topics, ghastly and grotesque are not on the menu as much as life in a besieged world, including the horror of everyday trauma, abuse, and inhumane people and systems.

"Evil" is a roiling slice of rock'n'punk, a flaring, charged affair that could easily have been a Turbonegro tune years later, apart from the momentary bursts of tight funk (a genre oddly relevant to much gothic music—just re-listen to Bauhaus). Above all, it commemorates dark wanderers—the punks and weirdos of L.A.'s seedy underbelly. "Black Cross" came closest to their hardcore brethren. It surges with blitzkrieg, manic tempos, abrupt time changes, and succinct

syncopation that marries the Minutemen with the Germs, whose Don Bolles drummed for 45 Grave and whose guitarist Pat Smear guest stars on a few tunes. Plus, it oozes with sinister cynicism and nihilism ("cancel the world / erase history") and employs a deft blend of uncanny and cryptic rhyme ("the users of the wheel, stink of oil and electric eels / users of forbidden tools we must be the fools").

"Wax" also takes aim at the feeling of inertia, emptiness, and stagnation that afflict

many people who end up lingering like hollow beings at the edge of obsolescence. The wax metaphor is pregnant with possibility. "Bent and lame / How unfortunate for me / I am just the same / A glob, a thing," Cancer bemoans, as if the human presence has dwindled into a mess of no meaning. And the song structure, again, employs twists and turns that are dynamic and propulsive, from thudding, droning funeral procession vibes to highly explosive measures of barely controlled mayhem. Though they sing unhesitatingly about the sour notes of life—"no flame, no light, no reflection, Waiting to die, just old wax . . . just old wax"—the song is an angry rebuttal to all that. Cancer's voice is vigor-infused. The sentiments spring into action and attempt to annihilate all the forces that turn people into such lame-feeling denizens of the void. The end-game is not sullenness and acquiescence; it is rebellion and rejection.

As a tough-as-nails punk poetess with a gothic wink, Cancer is an agent calling for a complete reversal of all such circumstances. Her scathing, caustic satires reclaim a sense of humanity. From such common wax, such mass-produced culture, she arose, too, creating a new code and animus. She became the unquiet woman that bowed to no misogynist shtick. That she did it with a horror vibe, via campy horror classics and Italian gore, makes it all the more engrossing as an artist.

Against Me!with Laura Jane Grace

The band that helped ignite the world's interest in Gainesville, FL, has run the gamut. They offer loose-knit, post-Fugazi, hoarse punk sing-alongs to tight-as-hell musical populism contextualized by abundant tattoos, and smart-ass stabs at left-wing clichés and conformity. They explore evocative and explorative narratives, as well as hook-savvy, fiery, propulsive, TNT-powered pop.

Whereas mainstream punk bands that sign to majors often end up over-cooked, bland, and faceless, Against Me! jumped ship after hitting number 34 on the Billboard charts and releasing two well-recevied records that did seem a bit too comfy, with slick studio production thanks to uber-alternative rocker producer Butch Vig. Once free, they kick-started their own studio Elkton and DIY label Total Treble Music while witnessing the transformation of former sandpaper-voiced singer Tom Gabel into the alluring and potent Laura Jane Grace. She, in turn, has become a multimedia fixture with a memoir, reality TV show, and her roots-rock band Laura Jane Grace and the Devouring Mothers.

The emotive album *Transgender Dysphoria Blues* by Against Me! featured a new rhythm section retrofitted by former members of Rocket from the Crypt (Herculean drummer Atom Willard) and The (International) Noise Conspiracy (fleet-footed Inge Johansson). The album quickly became not only a conceptual wake-up call to issues of gender fluidity in the modern era, it also unleashed new and revitalized music territories germane to the bold subject matter. As such, the narratives capture the voice of characters attempting to un-hitch and live untrammeled by a confusing past while reshaping an identity in the mottled glare of spotlights. The album is rife with powerful tunes: the marshaled Johnny Cash-gone-punk skitter rhythm of the title track; big fuzzed-out anthemic melodies ("True Trans Soul Rebel"—not far removed from their earlier tune "Americans Abroad"); slow howls underscoring the need to cut loose the pain and creeps of a former life, ("Black Me Out"); and soaring early Cheap Trick style rock'n'roll walls-of-sound ("Unconditional Love"), which nearly propels audiences to bounce floors to pieces. Other tunes are acerbic back-to-basic punk evocations of outsiderness ("Drinking with the Jocks"); cryptic and thrusting prog metal ("Osama Bin Laden as the Crucified Christ"); and a *Late Show With David Letterman* tested tune exploring the desire to live bravely with bite, honesty, openness, candidness, and purpose ("Fuckmylife666"). Such breathless material emanates from a constantly shifting, hungry, and iconic band.

Onstage in Houston in 2014, the band planted no stage banners, expressed no fuss over the fans tumbling onto the claustrophobic stage, and expressed no feigned sincerity, easily revealed by their network of broad smiles and banter. Such gigs felt like a private homecoming unleashing years of pent-up, riotous passion evoked by music as both pure adrenalized pleasure and a barometer of emboldened conscience. It occurred in an era when youth were too often stereotyped as overly intoxicated by a digital world, yet the band exuded a feral sense of the body electric, a fleshy reminder of humanity in flux.

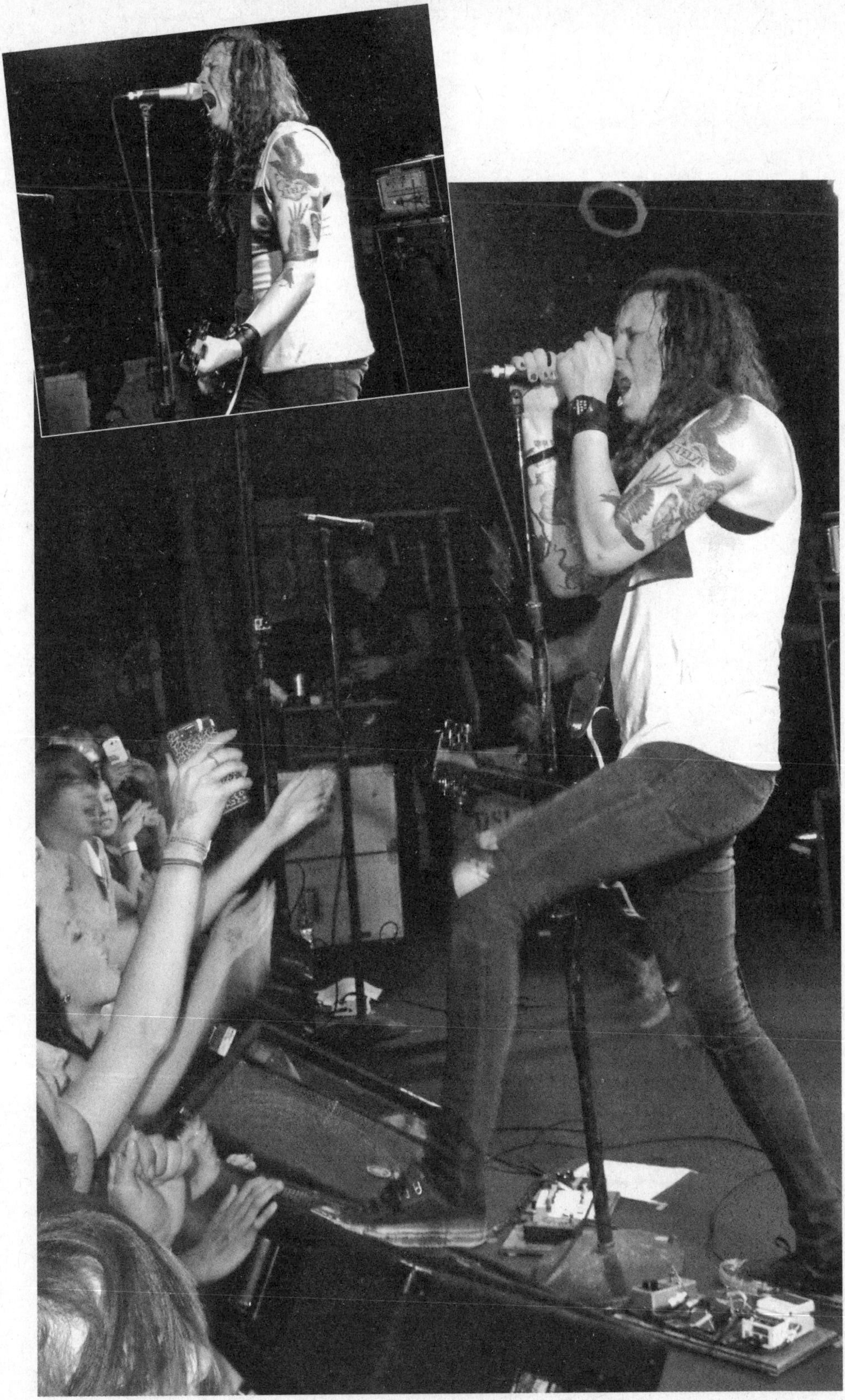

Against Me!, Houston, 2014, by David Ensminger

SHORT CUTS

The B-Girls

Unfortunately, these Toronto girls relentlessly got the short end of every showbiz stick and only released one slab of vinyl, care of über-pop godfather Greg Shaw.

Too bad all those dates opening for the Clash, Ramones, and Johnny Thunders, hanging in the studio with Blondie (check out their backing vocals on *Autoamerican*), and sharing plates of food with the New York Dolls didn't rev up cocaine-enthralled record reviewers and radio DJs enough to appreciate and launch forth their Go-Go's style lean punk pop. Check out songs like the urgent, hectic, totally catchy "B'Side" and the enthralling, pump-your-fist-in-the-air, emboldened "Who Says Girls Can't Rock," and what should be the anthem of the rock'n'roll tribe: "Dad thinks I should wear a dress." Oh, such old men—rickety staid fools with lead for a backbone!

Lucasta   Xenia   Cynthia

If you demand something even wilder, check out their live version of "Chinese Rocks," which foreshadows the 5,6,7,8's madcap Japanese-bred garage rock of the coming years.

Patti Smith

P atti Smith has been regarded as the high priestess poet of punk since she mingled Beatnik spiels with visionary outsider rock'n'roll at St. Mark's Church in New York City. Her "comeback" in the 1990s, most noticeably *Gone Again*, is a stunner replete with enduring insight and pointed passion backdropped by deaths of family and friends. The album proved she was trans-generational, and she has continued in full force ever since, penning books like *Just Kids* and *M Train* with literary acumen and insight.

Her output has remained steadfast and appealing, including her surprisingly laidback but nuanced tribute to titans like Jimi Hendrix, the Doors, Rolling Stones, and Nirvana on *Twelve* in 2007, but *Radio Ethiopia* is her misunderstood opus. To me, it is the gem to measure up to. The sonorous working class hymn "Pissing in the River," the rousing "Pumping," the shuddering helter skelter dissonance of the title track, and the lulling testimonial "Ain't It Strange" encapsulate Smith's unconventional possession of songcraft. Her voice is a vehicle for spirit caravans, and her personal testimonies of pain and regeneration, rage and renewal, and seduction and soul mining remain potent. Me writing about her is like taking on the *Old Testament*. Part of her will always remain unknowable, transcendent, and mysterious . . .

LiliPUT /Kleenex

L ong live the foreign invaders of punk prowess. LiliPUT/Kleenex easily proved that punk's switchboard could be turned on anywhere in the world, even the frozen climates of Switzerland, where it slew doldrums and sexism with its fierce brand of anxious, shrill, fierce, and sometimes screeching pop-punk. "Ü" feels like a Dada-poem set to riffs by a 1960s frat rock band, though with brittle aluminum guitar. The group's penchant for minimal one-word song titles is legendary ("Nice," "You," "Igel," "Türk," "Krimi"), as if punk songwriters lacked the time or patience to squander syllables on unnecessary writerly verbosity.

Atomized anarchic urges such as "Split" unload plentiful noise partly indebted to the style of Lora Logic. "Ain't You" echoes Crass during its femme powerhouse *Penis Envy* period, while the trebly "Madness" feels like a long lost relative to Sleater-

Kinney. Spewing out songs that seem to jostle the hard, gray, empty streets of its homeland with pulsing panic rhythms and righteous inflammatory anger, this band resembles a rock 'n' roll decontrol project with concept-art winks. Meanwhile, for some easygoing, almost nursery-like gibberish, "When the Cat's Away" is playful and free-spirited, while the taut, jittery "Thumblerdoll" awakens dance floors with barely disguised surf-punk.

The Slits

The enduring legacy of the Slits represents one of the most shambolic, dizzyingly unkempt, and alluringly anarchic of the first wave of British punk that re-molded the parameters of pop music. They effortlessly combined equal portions of raw echoey dance floor reggae and dub, bursting tribal-stomp beats, exploding punk shards, updated vaudevillian wit, and even American soul classicism. Even the sweet sounds of Marvin Gaye's "Heard It Through the Grapevine" are hybridized into messy jungle freneticism and warped vocals. From "Shoplifting" to "Typical Girls," the Slits set in motion a whole female-punk aesthetic that critics still debate. They offered an inchoate incomplete style, perfect imperfection, and a Do-It-Yourself amalgam all rendered with artful finesse.

For sure, their method is their madness. They delivered punk hits with delivering slanted and enchanted modes. If underground music ever needed a muse that reified, collapsed, smashed, and reinvented inherited musical genres, the Slits were the spear and spirit. Long live Ari Up, who died in 2010 but was immortalized in the song by No Love Less (half-penned by me!) called "Invasion" : "motherland to London clubs / mud caked albums brought the flood . . . " After their deluge, nothing was quite the same.

Vicky Satterwhite

Originally hailing from Corpus Christi (where her barely teenage band Slushi released a 7" single), Vicky Satterwhite became a venerable part of the late 1990s/early 2000s pop-punk scene that ballooned in Houston at clubs like Fitzgeralds and Instant Karma. In fact, I first met her at a pizza party for Jimmy Eat World before they shook the stage at Fitz's (an incisive, powerful gig before they became radio fodder). She effortlessly combined both the assertiveness and feminist consciousness of bands like Bikini Kill and Huggy Bear with the lighthearted flair of bands like the Go-Go's and B-52's, and explored oozing garage punk raucousness in bands like London Girl (who toured the West Coast) and the GiGi's. In addition, she has made fanzines, flyers, and album art for bands like 500 Mega Tons of Boogie. She has also shown paintings at galleries Diverse Words and Blaffer. In 2015, she won teacher of the year at Manvel High School, and she continues to perform with London Girl for reunions. With loads of natural sharp-witted intelligence fused with a Scottish rebellious streak, and always peppered with a boisterous sense of humor, she is both a music nut and comic nerd, an unparalleled teacher and effusive personality that helped plow infectious pop music back into the local Houston punk DNA.

London Girl, Houston, by Greg Rabel

Vicky says...

hat I always found so empowering about punk was the variety. Don't get me wrong, it could be far more diverse in gender, race, and size, but the openness and the acceptance of fellow punks always enticed me into the scene.

Early on, I noticed that women who did not fit in the sexy, stereotypical lead singer cliché had success based on their musical prowess in punk. I was crazy inspired by the Riot Grrrl movement as well as young punk priestesses like Poly Styrene from X-Ray Spex and Debora Iyall from Romeo Void. These ladies gave me strength.

Punk was safe for me as a young, plus-sized female. Here my voice and words mattered. The bands I was in were judged on our musical worth, not criticized on how I looked. I could feel sexy in my skin or smart in my skin and people still sang along and cheered us on. This was vital in building me as a person, and I am so thankful that I was completely empowered because of it.

Allison Gibson

ibson graduated from the HCC Coleman College for Health Sciences and is a bona fide heralded veteran of the underground Houston rock'n'roll community. She first came to prominence in bands like Manhole, a rare all-female sludge-rock unit in mid-1990s Houston that skirted the musical boundaries of grunge, punk, gunk, and heavy metal in the wake of notorious bands like dizzying L7. She then became part of DollyRockers and C'mon C'mon.

More recently, though, she has continued to be a deadly leading light as the intense, tattoo-etched, scorching vocalist of a few mainstays—thunder-clap Supergrave, Merkava, and Baron Von Bomblast. She embodies the power and persistence of women within the often male-dominated, dude-saturated, beard-soaked, harder-edged genres of music. Few people have the deep commitment, crazy work ethic, and longstanding no-bullshit attitude.

A Chat with Allison

My journey with the Houston music scene started around 1992, when I had just moved to Texas and was sniffing out the local metal and punk scenes. I ended up at some random keg party full of mohawks and skinheads and struck up a conversation with some people who were discussing getting bands together.

I had never sung before, but I had always wanted to. Blondie and Black Flag had already secured that idea long before I had reached that chance encounter. A guy named Damon, who I found out sang for Dixie Waste (and would later give Manhole its very first show at Pik'n'Pak), told me about an all-girl group who was forming but still needed a singer. He gave me the info of where they practiced and told me I should go by and check it out. I did.

A total stranger knocked on their door that day and asked to try out. Manhole was born. The next 13 or so years were a wild ride for me.

I'd never been in a band, I'd never played a show, I'd never "been on the road," I'd never met so many incredible people all doing what we were doing. Everything we did was amazing to me. It was all a new trip, a new experience.

Merkava, Houston, by David Ensminger

A total enlightenment. I learned quickly that with a female band, people either love ya or hate ya. There's no real middle ground there. I could be standing in a room of men sporting the biggest set of balls out of everyone and still be dismissed as a "wimpy chick" singer.

Or I could be commanding an audience of over a thousand and have every single person's undivided attention.

It was a coin toss.

I learned fast as well that Houston musicians don't fuck around much when it comes to writing and being on stage. Everybody is all in.

You have to be hardcore. You have to work your fifty hour work week and get on a stage on Friday night already tired and sore in an un-air-conditioned warehouse at 103 degrees and sweat and play your heart out and bleed into your whiskey . . . . That's how it's done here.

It's all anchors away or take your ship to a different sea because Houston musicians, in all of their glorious sloppy twang chord face assaulting rhythms, don't fuck around.

I was taught that from the get-go.

The other women I grew up with, my "lady rocker family," have always been so supportive. We push and empower each other to do incredible things and stand up for incredible causes.

They taught me, if you have a voice, to use it well. I feel incredibly lucky to have been all the places I've been. I've sang for rockabilly bands, played bass in an industrial project, screamed punk rock, and howled heavy metal until my throat went hoarse. I couldn't have done all that if I wasn't surrounded by people who support the creative spark that life gives us. I'll never stop playing music.

It's not a choice. It's in my blood, who I am, a lifeline to deal with misery and pain but also to embrace joy. Music is all, it's my everything. And I'll breathe it till the day my heart decides it's had enough of this world.

The 5678s

As many know, the Japanese underground remains a vibrant place to find American garage punk rejuvenated and re-invigorated, with a frenzied insta-trash twist. This disorderly trio, manic and maniacal for the last 25 years, is like a heavy dose of adrenaline that never dissipates. Perhaps best known for guest appearing in Quentin Tarantinos' *Kill Bill* film cranking out the adrenalized "I'm Blue" (by the Ikettes) and the borderline slo-mo psychobilly "I Walk Like Jayne Mansfield," the 5678s are much more than kitschy fodder for cinema. They truly represent bona fide roots rock ribaldry and raucous reinvention, from the wild, twangy surf of "Jane in the Jungle" to the rolling thunder and cat scratch vocals of "Guitar Date."

Of course, they offer up more languid fare for the beach jet-set, such as the oozing, Shirelles-inspired "Dream Boy" and "It's Rainy," which allow listeners to tiptoe into intimate dances. They also pay fiery homage to their faves, like the boisterous "Hanky Panky," distortion-drenched "Green Onion," and unbound "Great Balls of Fire." By walloping listeners with nitroglycerin-laced numbers like "Hey! Mashed Potato, Hey!" and the rockabilly riot "(I'm orry Mama) I'm a Wild One," they make rock 'n' roll feel ductile and ageless, like a time-out-of-time formula for fun.

Bikini Kill

As an accidental leader of the Riot Grrrl movement, Bikini Kill's reputation often preceded them, but the group's records document its full-bore commitment to creating crunchy, anthemic, and swaggering punk rock.

Bikini Kill offered old-school lyrical venom indebted to X-Ray Spex and the Runaways (surfacing on their tune "Rebel Girl," produced by Joan Jett), gender-minded politics, queer agitation, and unwavering commitments to DIY roots. Even playground chants morph into fierce onslaughts ("Demirep"), while slower dirge-pop outings like "Feels Blind" hint at restless visions.

Though their *Revolution Girl Style Now!* certainly inspired a whole generation to cut'n'paste fanzines, rent halls, grasp guitars, and fight the power of hegemony and dominant culture norms, the band was also a rockin' tour de force that summoned talent, resilience, and riotousness in an indelible mix. Bikini Kill's post break-up bands, like singer Kathleen Hanna's venture Le Tigre and The Julie Ruin, also evoke bracing and inventive soundscapes, but they never quite conjure the same vein-bursting thrills.

Bikini Kill in Minot, North Dakota 1994 by Brent Braniff

164

Gore Gore Girls

Even as Riot Grrrl held the media's attention, bustling and bristling female garage rock was plundering the world one dirty chord at a time. Gore Gore Girls brought the best out of their Detroit environs. Perhaps one of the greatest underrated garage bands on the planet, they emoted 1960s pop charm and panache, Detroit mayhem rooted in bands like the Stooges and MC5, and wily Tina Turner soulfire. To balance light bubblegum AM radio fare like "All Grown Up," they unleashed the grind of "Pleasure Unit," the guitar attack of hip-swaying "Casino" and "Voodoo Doll," and the swaying soft punch of "So Sophisticated."

Their fuzz-rock "Little Baby" was made for sweaty dance floors teeming with drippy hair pomade, tarnished clothes, and sloshy Budweiser. Cheeky, retro, and rootsy, they produced airtight Yardbirds-inspired instrumental jams like "Hammer Stomp" at the drop of a hat. "Loaded Heart" pumps with heavy riffage, whoopass soul-punk urges, and soaring back-up vocals, while the slow fuzz stomper "You Lied to Me Before" reeks of salty leather and murky nightclubs where pained lovers bury miseries in dusty records and empty glasses.

The Lunachicks

The Lunachicks were a peculiar New York City breed of punk that looked back to grimy Gotham, channeled the likes of Wendy O. Williams (the Plasmatics), and foreshadowed the punk-as-camp style of Hedwig and the Angry Inch and the Toilet Boys. They never offered a stripped-down punk Ramones formula; instead, single songs like

"FDS" wielded muscular rock 'n' roll, operatic gestures, scat and funk vocals, and psychedelic guitar interludes.

As such, the Lunachicks were a prime pastiche of cunning power, strong smoldering style, humor and jest, and dramatic speed and thrust. While the Riot Grrrls were making manifestos, the Lunachicks were donning wacky outfits, making records jocular as comic books, reeking like the Dictators on methamphetamine, and scaring the hell out of people expecting cliché underground rock babes.

Sure, both schtick and shock-value undercoated their stabs at punk fame, but they certainly packed heavy-duty musical pistons under their hood, proving they were as skilled, aggro, and sly as any other act occupying the city's tough streets.

Slant 6

Featuring members of the Washington D.C. gem Autoclave, Slant 6 was a tuneful titan of punk's third wave just as its label Dischord Records became home base to more "mature" post-punk outfits, such as Jawbox, Holy Rollers, and their predecessor Fire Party. Yet the group embodies a haunting reverse invasion of culture by delivering gutted rock 'n' roll as one-part homage to the

bands it was reared on while making the retrofitted music feel genuine, disassembled, and filtered through new webs of experience. The stripped down, cutting "Babydoll" pops and punches, becoming agile, destructive, mad, and fixating at times.

Slant 6 operate in svelte mode, reinforcing clear-cut formulas, similar to many garage punkers, but they transmit artful adaptations with spry surges, keen authenticity, and restless reclamation. Sometimes the tunage is vexing ("Retro Duck") or bare-knuckled jazz-noise ("Inzombia"), but Slant 6 also offers up the choppy, primal, and perfectly quirky "Don't You Ever" and swelling, upheaving "What Kind of Monster Are You?". In all, they create a power trio antidote to East Coast math rock. And Myra Powers continues her onslaughts in bands like Thee Thee's, whose bareboned, tumbledown tunes like "Shiny" remain committed to antsy, lo-fi garage rock.

Exene (Christine) Cervenka of X, Knitters, Auntie Christ, and more

John Doe and Exene Cervenka were like a roughed-up punk version of Sonny and Cher, playing their rough'n'ready, literate, and lurid Los Angeles noir punk with vintage hummable melodies, earnest political potency, and easy-on-the-ear thrust. Though her voice has never been pitch-perfect, Exene armed it with plenty of desire, capturing the tone and timbre of punk's insurgent smartness and artful angst.

After ricocheting against John Doe in tunes like "Ridin With Mary" and melding with him on

pivotal tracks like "Hungry Wolf" and later tuneage like "I'm Lost," she shed that skin for young gun projects like Auntie Christ and the Original Sinners, only to return to her roots again. Her wily poetry and visionary, Latin-influenced mixed media collages remain vital as well. She remains the limber backbone of punk, providing creative DNA for the movement since the 'zero hour.'

The Bags with Alice Bag/Alicia Armendariz

If you think hardcore punk was paved by solely by bands like the Bad Brains, then switch gears for a moment and listen to the Bags' blitzkrieg on "We Will Bury You" and especially "Survive," with its classic tempo-twitching build-up to blast-off beats. Explosive and androgynous, Bag defined the 'terrible beauty' of punk women who struggled at home, at the work place, in the neighborhoods, and the punk clubs. She was the voice of refusal and resistance.

As a feminist punk singer for the Bags who chose "shock-level" approaches that mixed art, music, and identity politics, she had one foot in punk sensibilities and one foot in Chicana culture. Her intense, vitriolic performances shattered gender assumptions about women during the halcyon era of soft adult pop music offered by the likes of Karen Carpenter and Carly Simon.

Undeterred even today, her blog *Diary of a Bad Housewife* features dozens of interviews with the women from punk's history, while her book *Violence Girl: East L.A. Rage to Hollywood Stage, a Chicana Punk Story* takes a deep, penetrating, renegade inner-view of the punk struggle for dignity and empowerment

In an article titled "Violence Girl" on her web site, she candidly explores how these multiple forces collided in her, instigating a kind of personal punk metamorphosis:

> All the violence that I'd stuffed down inside of me for years came screaming out . . . all anger I felt towards people who had treated me like an idiot as a young girl because I was the daughter of Mexican parents and spoke broken English, all the times I'd been picked on by peers because I was over-weight and wore glasses, all the impotent rage that I had towards my father beating my mother just exploded.

BAGS

NO EXCESS BAGISIMS

The multiplying, disheartening Otherness—the sense of gender exclusion and disparity; the sense of domestic violence and family breakdown; the anguish of an imperfect body in a country manifesting plastic perfection; and the immigrant dream meeting prejudice heads-on—became distilled into the punk body, a site of negation.

In addition, she has been a decades-long activist who has focused on geo-political issues like revolutions in Central America—first doing benefits for CISPES, then working alongside Sandinistas in liberated Nicaragua—to date-rape culture here at home, releasing singles like "No Means No" to bring awareness to the issue.

X-Ray SpeX with Poly Styrene /Marianne Joan Elliott_Said

This cutting-edge band is best known for their brand of saxophone-doused punk that mixed brute musical naivety with trenchant wit and street savvy feminism. Styrene, daughter of a displaced Somali aristocrat, whose voice Greil Marcus compared to a toilet disinfectant, notoriously spooked Johnny Rotten (Sex Pistols) with her hallucinations. Her tumbling, harrowing vocals on "I Am a Cliche" are like university lectures on deconstruction boiled down to haiku-like intensity ("I am a cliche / pink is obscene").

In other songs like "The Day the World Turned Dayglo," Styrene's assured lyrical phrasing interrogates the vacuumed corridors of the bourgeoisie, including the supermarket glares, "artificial" living, genetic engineering, and the pretexts of comfort without satisfaction. As such, Styrene used her voice as a weapon—fragmenting the mid-1970s doldrums of a passive, self-satisfied world—and created a codex for living in the age of commodity-hypnotized consumer culture surrounded by the sheen, gloss, and ultimate fakeness of adverts. Yes, "The Day the World Turned Dayglo," with its soft, lulling melodies full of deodorants, clean teeth, and antiseptics, is all that and more. She truly was a "Warrior in Woolworths."

The Raincoats

Most notably, their use of rustic stringed instruments, including violins foreshadowing the Mekons' 1980s ventures, and off-kilter vocal harmonizing, is truly bracing and perfectly bound to their rushed ramshackle pop and Velvet Underground frenetic noise grooves. In that vein, the Raincoats proved they were inventive enough to find potency in past and present eras. They never killed their idols: they re-invented them, like their wistful basement punk-funk exploration of the Kinks' gender-bending classic rocker "Lola."

With plentiful smarts, they wielded powerful anti-rockers like "Fairytale in the Supermarket," easily drifted into arty netherworlds in "You're a Million" and "Family Treet," and brandished skittering dub on "Baby Song." But they never felt overly pretentious and unwieldy. One could dance and gyrate to "Balloon/Balloonacy" or zone out to the jazzy "Rainstorm," content that boredom was not on the menu during a fitful session with this band.

Siouxsie Sioux/Susan Janet Ballion

Few punks on the planet have aged so gracefully as Siouxsie Sioux/Susan Janet Ballion of Siouxsie and the Banshees, who cut a presence on the scene that was/is indomitable, singular, and achingly cool. She feels somewhere between Kabuki and a wolverine. She is shadowy and severe, elegant and elegiac, hypnotic and heroic, and she later exhibited stellar pop star flair but remained aloof and anti-pop too. She lives as multiples: part Creature, part Banshee, part dark-haired photogenic raven of the goth void, part ambassador of high art. She made music that felt here and now, yet rooted in a divine spirit teleported from the attic of the past.

Almost anyone even slightly alternative can hum one song by the Banshees, a provocative outfit that never fit any one genre-defining category. They mutated from blistering, unflinching art-punk to eerie dark wave sensibilities, then switched again and delivered dance-pop with shimmering perfection. Sioux's emotive voice is hard to shake off. Her drummer and future husband supplied the supple percussive backbeats, and the band's guitar work—willowy, searing, and sly—lingers today even in the bombast of the Killers. Try something mid-period, like the atmospheric "Arabian Nights," breathless and tumbling "Spellbound," poetic and incandescent "Into the Light," or biting and haunting "Halloween."

Kira Roessler of Black Flag and Dos

I n the heyday of American hardcore, Kira was the (un)femme icon of Southern California punk style, with limber, well-honed fingers dancing across the strings, creating a solid but molten groove that sliced through the prog-noise [169] barrage of Greg Ginn in Black Flag. She stood defiant as punk crowds jeered and chewed through their own fantasies or bullshit sexism, and her work with Dos proved she had a nuanced jazz streak in her as well.

She played with notable others too, like DC3, but songs like Flag's infectious "Black Coffee" showcase her prowling, thudding, and unrelenting mid-paced dexterity that led the way for stoner rock bands like Nebula and Fu Manchu.

Along with women playing in bands like the Dicks, Sado-Nation, Sin 34,

and Capitol Punishment, she proved hardcore was not merely a testosterone-charged boys' club but a potential level playing field for women with guts, determination, and savvy doses of intelligence. Her current work as sound editor proves her craft is still alive and well. This email exchange with me first surfaced in *Left of the Dial.*

LOTD: At Black Flag practices, you once said in an interview, Greg Ginn could go for ten hours while the rest of you would drop out one by one.

Kira: Well, bass and drums are more physical than guitar, if you ask me. And sometimes I think that it is the one area where being female may be a factor. The muscle structure in my hand can only be built up so far. The concept of having someone's large hands attached to my arms was a fantasy during Black Flag . . . I have to practice, I have to warm up before gigs, I have to make the parts become somewhat automatic to my hands, or I will suck. There are those who may not need that much work. I am not one of them. Maybe that is true for all instruments. My hand will seize and not move the way I tell it to if I don't warm up before a gig.

LOTD: Do you feel it was important to Black Flag that people saw you as a "journeyman" of sorts?

Kira: Girls grow up as tomboys all the time and always have, and they would naturally always participate in music and sports in garages and playgrounds . . . Mo Tucker is a

Black Flag, Houston, by Ben DeSoto

172

good example, and there are many we haven't heard from. There is no obstacle in the playing, in the interest, the capacity, and the role, sex symbol or otherwise.

Sleater Kinney

Guitarist/singer Carrie Brownstein has to be one of the most cerebral people in punk (check out her memoir *Hunger Makes Me a Modern Girl*). She is as well-spoken, self-reflective, meta-cognitive, earnest, and intellectual as she is ironic and hilarious on the sketch comedy show *Portlandia*.

Even if you deplore the band, Sleater-Kinney has forged an irascible, deft style, creating a singular musical trajectory that made a whole generation of writers swoon along with the audiences. Even the group's mid-period work *The Woods* retained plenty of efficacy, supple textures, and unbridled diversity, as did their newest slab *No Cities to Love*.

Yes, Bikini Kill produced frenetic Riot Grrrl templates, but this trio, spanning three decades, committed long and hard to its unconventional blend of frenzied vocals, antsy twist-n-turn drumming, curlicuing guitars, and anything-goes structure. Early fare like "Dance Song '97" feels like a pumped-up, scalding version of LiliPUT and Kleenex; meanwhile, the slightly Kim Gordon shaded "Get Up" is moody and mercurial, and the band's layered, soaring, and terrifying beauty "Jumpers" offers swaying lulls and explosity in equal measure. "One Beat" feels like a percussion-drenched literary duel between singers Corin Tucker and Brownstein. The often sizzling yet perennially focused unit always felt like it was on the verge of vanishing into its own brand of inventiveness.

The BellRays with Lisa Kekaula

The BellRays, featuring husband-wife duo Bob Vennum and Lisa Kekaula, are a seminal, fiery rock'n'roll band that have criss-crossed the ever-changing country for decades. Unfazed, they remain defiantly excellent, as if a sustained force that fuses together the promise of rock'n'roll as both liberty-defining and sweat-inducing—like the groovy romp found on even their newest outing *Punk Funk Rock Soul Vol II* (Honeypot Records), including the forceful crunch of "Love and Hard Times" and the seductive slow blues whir of "Every Chance I Get." Singer Lisa Kekaula, who is part African-American and Hawaiian, stands and delivers. Her roots-deepened, hair-tingling, whiplash soul taps into punk's nervy force and rigor.

BellRays, Houston, 2002, by David Ensminger.

Though left out of most histories of punk (an act that is baffling and prejudiced), black women have remained an intrinsic part of the core: the Controllers and X-Ray Spex in the 1970s; Mutley Chix and Fire Party in the 1980s; plus Tribe 8 and the BellRays in the 1990s and beyond. But Kekaula has gained more notoriety by appearing on tunes by inventive house music masters Basement Jaxx and electronic cognoscenti the Crystal Method. Incredible dynamism and dizzying power are the propellants behind the BellRays, who remain a quintessential squad that converges dizzying Detroit rock'n'roll licks (à la the Stooges) and vintage scorcher Tina Turner with AC/DC (whose "Highway to Hell" the BellRays zealously cover), erupting in a blast of guitar rumble, battering ram drums, and coiled bass. Kekaula's frenetic, deep-throated, wailing roots-gone-punk vocals are a mighty force of untamed nature. And, just as Kekaula regularly touts from stage, "This is a rock show!" the band becomes a wall-of-sound that proves just that. For years, the BellRays stuck to a pared-down, no-frills, close to the ground recording style. On the album *Let it Blast*, that meant recording in a 15 x 15 room with a Sansui 6-track. While this teemed with lo-fi, Do-It-Yourself merits, their revved-up polemics—a flare for confrontation (like tackling the Ku Klux Klan on "Evil Morning" from *Grand Fury*) and soulful exhortations to be strong and confident—always feel both resilient and personal. Meanwhile, their tunes also feel sinewy and singularly honed, like a reflex, as if they are attempting to

175

crush the glossy corporate appeal of modern music meant for elevator rides. "It was never our intent in any of those incidences to be like, no, man, we should just go all-out DIY and do it that way," admits Kekaula to me on the phone. "We were just working within our means. I think we've always been that band. So even though this time we were able to get things recorded with Jim Diamond, from Ghetto Recorders studio, unfortunately my voice was not in good shape when we went and did the initial tracks. So, a bunch of that stuff we had to bring home and make it shine and glow . . . That's part of our DIY thing, where we just figure out; alright, this isn't the perfect surroundings we thought we were going to have, to be able to cut the record and be done with it, but I think some of the songs grew because we were able to do that too." All of their music feels pressed with that can-do spirit and grit. For instance, "One Big Party" and "Too Many Houses in Here" are akin to an updated MC5 track that rocks wide-open, wild-style, and careening; meanwhile "Tell the Lie" lets loose a funk-punk platter and "Get on Thru" pegs a Chuck Berry style while adding mighty wallops and wails. The railing "Snotgun" focuses on the fight for freedom while being wedged between Crips, Aryans, and the FBI. On *Black Lightning*, they reached new heights behind slicker production, straightened song structure, and honed soulcraft, including the title song's titular evocation of "raw power in your veins." Furthermore, "Sun Comes Down" dances in

BellRays Houston, 2002, by David Ensminger.

a Motown sway, replete with strings, snare rimshots, and lyrical postcards of sundown and romance. Any sensible revolution must have a soundtrack that recognizes dance as the human condition and voices that are real and authentic. "There is so much stuff out there these days that is created," explained Kekaula, "even great voices that have been morphed and changed, so you don't really hear the quality of it. I want the whole reality of it. We do what we do in a very stripped down fashion . . . there is a truth in us being able to do it [that way] . . . . It might not be trendy, it might not be these other things, and there may not be a ton of people out there telling you this the greatest shit, but we know it is." Across their song spectrum, "Power to Burn" is an anthemic surge, rich in choruses, evoking tropes of the road ahead, while "Living a Lie" is an outsider ode that describes the difficulty of cutting a markedly different path from corporate pretenders—the faux-hearted heavies that inundate the airwaves. Then, the unexpectedly uplifting bounce-beat "The Way" sounds cut in Memphis, as if a 45 rpm platter perfectly square with the Stax Records roster. In the last few years, their *Punk Funk Rock Soul* offered toughened rock-alongs like "Mine All Mine," which should have caused a million fist pumps in the air as the narrator tries to recover from "the hole inside where soul should be." Spiels like "Shake Your Snake," funk-merited à la Sly and Family Stone, resonate with a syncopated groove fashioned around the invocation "left, right, shake" that separates "the men from the mammals." Infectious and limber, it curlicues around a slithering beat, while "I Don't Wanna Cry" bemoans lost love that results from mistaking

BellRays, Houston, 2002, by David Ensminger

money and material goods for acts of affection. Blaring organ, soaring vocals, and a thumping backbeat create a backdrop to the weary heart thrown down on the ground. In all, across 30 EPs, singles, and albums released by myriad small and smaller labels, they have remained a battering ram against homogenization, a symbol of convergence culture, and a tribute to the spirit of keeping music divorced from the dumbed-down, devouring jaw of corporate entities. "Hallelujah," you might find yourself saying in the heat of Rudyards while watching rock'n'roll get saved one song at a time. "I think anytime we would make a record, to me," says Kekaula, "That is what I was trying to do when I am singing it. It's just not for me, you know. I got what I need. I am trying to give it to everyone else."

The Elected Officials with Sophie Rousmaniere

The Elected Officials, a blistering and fiery politico-punk band led by filmmaker and singer Sophie Rousmaniere, now has ten years under their belt. To celebrate, they released *Death For Sale* in 2020 to highlight their brand of relentless agitation. Of course, that unfolded under the

duress of a bitter presidential campaign and the even greater distress and disruption caused by COVID-19, the virus pandemic threatening life daily.

With members brought together from over a dozen previous bands, the Elected Officials are a brash, potent, hectic, and fervent anarcho-political force whose members straddle Texas and New Mexico. Their typical targets are not just the machinations and madness of greedy, toxic corporations, consumer-society, and not-so-hallowed religion; they also focus on everyday people's DIY efforts to rebuild their future based on both resistance and participation. In doing so, Rousmaniere encourages talk but lionizes action even more. The band has also tapped into modern media with energy and focus, creating videos not just of band life and their products, but broader issues, including Native American social justice and beyond.

Rousmaniere, a jack-of-all-trades, came to being in a band in a roundabout way. "I have always been a producer of something, like film festivals and documentaries. I had a punk bar and tattoo shop in Thailand twenty years ago. I have been a body piercer trained by the best there is. I am about as ADHD too as it gets, so yeah, I've been a journalist, importer, non-profit organizer, jewelry maker, booking agent, film producer, hotelier, band manager, writer, mom, vocalist, and political organizer. I think this ties back into how I feel when I am in the developing world. I don't feel the need to be so productive I want to tear my hair out. I've been infested by the productivity virus—American concepts of validating yourself with more accomplishment. But, alas, it has gotten me to where I want to be: producing with Grimace Records and Issue TV, on stage with MDC (as sometimes co-singer) and the Elected Officials, and raising a beautiful eight-year-old girl."

In Trumpian times, when sides have been polarized, moods darkened, and lurking violence is potentially possible around every comment and glare, the band harnesses discontent, hooks some humor to it, and places it into a global vision of people struggling for change. It is the sound of empowerment unfolding, like a battle cry for social and environmental justice, a call to action against corporate malfeasance, as well as a full-throated campaign for restored democratic rights in an era marked by Republican voter suppression.

The Elected Officials produce gritty hardcore punk, emblematic on forceful tunes likes "The Lobby," which takes a swing at the National Rifle Association. Others bemoan the impending disaster of radiation, like "Fallout," which delivers a blend of Discharge and Dead Kennedys—if they each had a face-contorting, bellowing female singer like Rousmaniere.

Yet, one of the dilemmas of playing such highly-charged and charred hardcore is that some participants may slam dance to the soundtracks but not muster enough energy to head to the polls. Some, in fact, are simply anti-system: they refuse to vote. Yet, for Rousmaniere, the issues are clear as ice.

"The reality of permanent destruction of habitats, species, war, oil spills, is hard to take," she says. "Taking responsibility can be even harder, and if you don't believe you can change anything, you definitely can't. I think punks sometimes like the idea of not being involved. It frees one from the responsibility of giving energy to a system that is broken and can't be fixed until a major makeover."

But that major makeover, which might have been possible under the dictates of left-winger Bernie Sanders or professorial Elizabeth Warren, fell flat with the general public in 2020.

"That does not mean we give up," Rousmaniere says. "Voting is something the suffragettes and people of color have fought for vigilantly. Our lyrics speak of a game of politics that we don't get to play. I will vote against the worst of whatever evil is in front of me. Politics is a messy game, and The Elected Officials simmer in our juices but always keep action, even any small kind, in our MO."

Electrical Officials, Houston, 2019. by David Ensminger

"Music, action, progress, no matter how small," she argues, is how the band survives and thrives in these days of tumult and friction.

Rousmaniere, who has made documentary films that address global issues—including the difficult lives of people fighting for daily dignity in parts of hard-pressed Africa—sings about "Toxic Shock," poisoned water, and the unlucky 99% who are barred from attaining much financial stability or opportunity. The Elected Officials seem to be "occupying" punk much like previous rebel heroes: akin to the modes and manners of previous bands such as M.D.C., D.O.A., and Conflict, their updated messaging is composed of more than lightning-fast d-beats, careening power chords, and guttural vocals.

"It's funny how to some people punk rock is just music. But it means so many things to us. We find ourselves playing in the sandbox with the other weirdos who espouse our own brand of revolutionary thought. For me, D.O.A. who are a self-proclaimed 'Protest band,' and others of their ilk, truly reflect my journey into punk rock. I was an activist before I was a punk. I would not have found the scene, except I too was angry and had no community."

In fact, Rousmanier was an outsider, even an outcast. "I didn't have punk friends, I was just pissed. Like many others, we found each other, which made us feel better about the harsh reality of the world." Punk became a conduit, a manner of networking, a platform, and a way to harness energies.

Having spent lengthy time abroad in Asia, Rousmanier sees conflict, struggle, and personal happiness very differently than somebody constantly attuned to Twitter feeds and the allure of algorithms in America.

"Even when facing major conflict and intense poverty, I see people in the Developing World smiling more than I see in Northern Europe or the U.S. In some of these places, it's like some people are born punk, fighting and pushing to survive, which has given them strength to fight for something better. Mexico, Indonesia, Brazil . . . all amazing punk scenes, amazing cultures rich with tradition."

In fact, Rousmaniere has spent the last few months in Mexico, where her band has toured as well.

"America does not create a culture of togetherness. The fact that we can isolate ourselves because we have wealth leads us toward unnatural ways of being. We concern ourselves with what is on TV versus the simple need to support basic human needs: the need to support each other in low-income communities brings a closeness that we don't have here."

Whereas in America, punk is an adhesive that binds a community, intense poverty may do the same elsewhere, with a punk subtext. "When there is no money, people still help neighbors," Rousmaniere explained to me. That route seems very Do-It-Together.

In the end, over the last decade, the Elected Officials have been writing lyrics that expose amassed corruption and bolster hope amid rampant fear. In doing so, they want everyone to understand that punk is not a commercial culture that wants to sell fans special VIP packages and costly tickets; instead, punk delves into community-building and preservation, from the ground up. It is a distinctly democratic force that "leads us to honoring people over profit," as Rousemaniere insists.

That reason alone should be enough to drive people to experience their gigs.

The Motels with Martha Davis

The Motels arrived onto the FM airwaves disguised as "new wave," but were truly a complicated post-punk band. Riveted by numerous line-up changes, the band has served to showcase the enduring croon, warm songwriting, and compelling character of singer and guitarist Martha Davis. She has remained the durable ballast in the band's tumultuous history.

Her vulnerability and strength seem to commingle on tunes like the brooding, atmospheric "Suddenly Last Summer" and the beloved "Only the Lonely" from their epic *All Four One* album, a titular tune for the

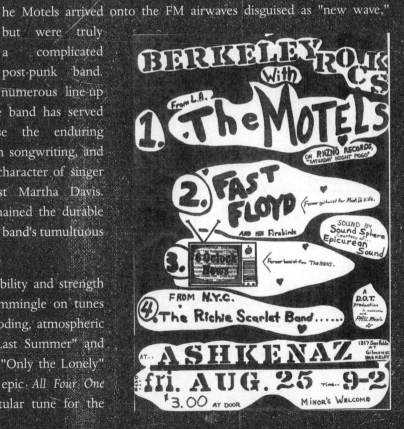

forlorn. And while Australia and France have embraced the band with unwavering support, much of America still looks at the band as a novelty, a 1980s holdover, even though Davis's immutable rock balladry offers well-tempered modes of mastery, especially on tunes like "Take the L."

The band, in various incarnations, has a curious past, first starting as Berkeley-goes-to-Los Angeles rockers in the early 1970s, under the name Warfield Foxes. However, as the band transformed into the Motels, they created a lasting impact as punk blossomed in its very earliest incarnations in the city. Their Do-It-Yourself tactics, common among bands like the Dogs and the Pop, caused tremors.

By the late 1970s, the band was making its round at clubs like Madame Wong's, carving tunes like the infectious, forceful, nimble "Kix," which asks, "What the hell do you do with the kids these days?" As a mother who raised her kids through persistence and public assistance, Davis's lyrics offer more than flimsy rhetoric.

Yet, the debut album's enduring imprint was "Total Disguise," which climbed the charts in Australia. It symbolized the band's persuasive, soulful plea for control in a fledgling world of uncertainties—bedrooms full of stained sheets, headaches, and inconsolable desire. Meanwhile, "Atomic Café" unleashed a soundtrack for the midnight clientele of perfumed neon wanderers experiencing "déjà vu" on the streets. Martha delivers lines like "The lonely ain't so free" so nonchalantly it slips under the skin like a virus. And "Porn Reggae" mashes up cabaret drama, tense and ductile reggae-syncopated leanings, and lover's rock'n'roll, similar to Elvis Costello. It's a riveting hybrid.

Like the Go-Go's, who once shared the infamous club the Masque as their practice space with them, the Motels began to chart and infiltrate mass pop consciousness. But while the Go-Go's served up a brazen youthfulness dolloped with surf-city relish, the Motels were mood-driven and studio-crafted, a late-night journey into near-fatal emotional collisions. In the case of their own surfside song, "Tragic Surf," they evoke a moonlight drowning (a "demon wave straight from hell").

In doing so, they offered a precise, sobering, and somber adult clarity—often tempered by moments of barely muted punk jolt and abrasive guitar—that signaled the vein of distress that runs through even their most subdued songs.

Their second album, *Careful*, is just as innovative. The murky, fuzzy "Danger," with its saxophone bursts and driving drums, cuts the same mood as mid-period Psychedelic Furs; it is not fiery music, but it is not adult-wave either. The dark currents of "Envy" offer an earful-of-warning, like a re-invented blues, bemoaning those who want the narrator's man and money with stirring musical break-outs.

Meanwhile, "Days Are O.K. (But the Nights Were Made for Love)" is an anthemic rouser with blipping keyboards that seems kindred to moments of power pop, while "Cry Baby" speeds through its wall of desperate feelings, ("What kind of fool am I? / I can't tell you goodbye"), in which the narrator attempts to reclaim self-esteem in the throes of displeasure, fallen light, and loneliness. The guitar solo—a noisy aggressive whir—feels like the collateral damage of digging deep in the psyche to find strength and solace when one becomes fragmented.

And as Blondie (who Motels resemble a bit on "Bonjour Baby") balanced accessible stylings with artful tendencies, the Motels did so on 1983's *Little Robbers*, with its knack for offering unblinking gazes at life and love gone wrong. In doing this, they honed big production around strong messaging on tunes like "Remember the Nights," with its soaring chorus and memory-tinged lyrics surrounded by hammering drums that were a little too slick for some.

The band, also known as Martha Davis and the Motels, has continued to capitalize on their strengths for the last few decades, even borrowing tunes from other notables like "Sweet Dreams (Are Made of This)" from the Eurythmics; "Nothing Compares to U" from Sinead O'Connor (originally written and performed by Prince); and even "Poker Face" by Lady Gaga.

Though these recordings are immensely enjoyable, her legacy is likely better served by her own personal solo work, including the moody, candid, sizzling guitar-driven allure of "Into Your Arms" ("allowed the luxury of distress / it's not really a crime"), which feels scruffy as a faded denim jacket. Or the humble "By the Fire," with its slow tides and piano that mills about the undercurrent.

And when she sings "I'm tired of the same old shit" on the electro-pulsing demo for her tune "Between the Sheets," she is not a woman seeking empty compliments, or the same denominations and routine. She is seeking a degree of definition about her role, her life, and her truth.

In her creative reach and identity, in her resilience and path forward, in her clear eyes that never stray too far from the trouble truths, in her grainy image of romance, in her beating fast heart and focus trained on our frailties, she cuts a clear channel through time and trends. She sings not only for the lonely, but also the spiritual textures of crude power play, whether in life, business, or the heart.

AFTERWORD
NEIGHBORHOOD BRATS AND PETROL
GIRLS: The Future is Now

This book was re-edited, re-designed, and finished with zeal and a labor of love as the pandemic shook the earth, sowing confusion, angst, risks, and death. I admit, at times, even with my own editors and staff, I became itchy and difficult, too-ready to push ahead.

Listening to a few bands helped sort my brain and sate my restless body. Yes, I dance, even alone.

Neighborhood Brats left me speechless when I saw them live in the spring of 2019. Tunes like "Late Stage Capitalism" made economic theory feel like a disheveled pogo party; the song decried the woes of the U.S. without leaving behind the jump, skitter, and rattle of rock'n'roll. Think MC5 meets the Adolescents, or an updated, female-power fueled Jerry Lee Lewis on the piano-bursting "Night Shift."

With total dedication to punk that pre-dates flimsy fads and subgenre compulsion, the Brats are simply a slice of West Coast tunefulness and menace, substance and soaring energy. Almost no singer on earth can equal the propelling acrobatic synergy of singer Jenny Angelillo, whose tattooed frame contorts into a thousand different shapes as she zigzags across puny stages as the music roars; meanwhile, her bellows buoy over the discordant guitar discharges. Live and loud, brisk and unbothered by hip factors, they charged ahead in 2021 on tunes like hard-hearted "I Want You" and the softer blow of "Who Took the Rain," which lands somewhere shy of late-period Dils, mixed with their own careening power pop.

Meanwhile, the Petrol Girls have also made me re-think the currency of music in a time of mass rebellion.

With chiseled vocal ferocity, an unbending dedication to the politics of self-liberation, multi-layered feminism, and a modern punk musical frame that exerts forceful tunefulness, Petrol Girl is utterly confrontational as they catalog the fucked-up dystopia called here and now. Resembling acts like Propagandhi, Strike Anywhere, Crass, and War on Women, they infuse pointed jabs into breathless lines like "Touch me again and I'll fucking kill you" while never relying on readymade, easily-stitched forms of assault.

In fact, emboldened with intelligence, their albums *Talk of Violence* (2016) and *Cut & Stitch* (2019) are emblems of resistance punching holes in the clean metal surface of Western modes. Their anger is not debased and debauched or merely cantankerous punk phlegm: it is unapologetic and unveils an acute dissection of values, mores, and customs that too often have a thin veneer of progressive tendencies hiding hard truths.

Cross-pollinated by members across Europe, but headquartered in London, they revere classic punk troublemakers like Poly Styrene (X-Ray Spex) while focusing on disassembling and dismantling control systems. Their narrative scope includes everyday, common personal territory, like refusing to be being quiet and say no, to system-wide issues of repression that are built-in throughout present day countries, sectors of life, and politico-economic webs.

To sum up their sheer bravado, imagine Gang of Four's sensibilities landing upon the charred landscape of modern hardcore.

Most importantly, these new bands, still active and energetic, truly embody the future of punk.

Index

THANK YOU TO

Maximum RocknRoll, Left of the Dial, Popmatters, Razorcake, Houston Press, David Lester, Jim Blanchard, Dischord Records, all the women that offered their writing and perspectives in this volume, Deborah Iyall for the ongoing encouragement, my sister Laura Patterson, and my first wife Aimee (Shields), who first prompted me to write at length.

Special Thanks to
My wife Julie, my constant lover, companion, sidekick,
partner in creative crimes, and office assistant,
who has remained the integral core of my productivity.

No Comet, Houston, 2016, by David Ensminger